TRUE FOUNDER

"*True Founder* is a must-read for aspiring entrepreneurs! Starting a business is hard, and Marc Lafleur does a great job of capturing the truth behind what it takes to be a successful first-time founder. If you want a leg up on the competition, *True Founder* serves as your tactical guide to getting started."

—Michele Romanow
Dragons' Den
CEO, Clearco

"This book was written by someone who has actually made money. These tips are real. Marc is an incredible business person who has strategies for first-time founders that are invaluable. It's a must-read if you're considering starting your own business, if you want to know tricks of the trade, or if you just want to be successful."

—Mikhaila Peterson
Host, *The Mikhaila Peterson Podcast*

"Any founder who is truly serious about taking their business to the next level must read *True Founder*. It's filled with valuable insights and lessons. No fluff or filler, only to the point, practical, and actionable takeaways that can be applied to nearly any business regardless of industry. After reading *True Founder*, I found myself immediately taking many of the valuable insights and putting them into action. Marc's journey of success from zero to a $16 million deal is broken down to the most critical lessons and learnings that any founder can relate and aspire to."

—Sheena Brady
Founder, Founders Fund

"*True Founder* is honest, entertaining, and practical. All first-time founders looking to get a sense of what their early years might look like will get tremendous value from this book. Marc Lafleur provides founders with actionable tips and tricks, all the while keeping readers engaged with his stories about the highs and the lows of building a $20 million business at the age of thirty."

—Giovanni Marsico
Founder, Archangel Academy

TRUE FOUNDER

TRUE FOUNDER

FOUNDER

What No One Else Has the Guts to Teach You
About Starting Your First Business

MARC LAFLEUR

Forbes | Books

Published by ForbesBooks, Charleston, South Carolina.
Member of Advantage Media Group.

ForbesBooks is a registered trademark, and the ForbesBooks colophon is a trademark of Forbes Media, LLC.

Printed in the United States of America.

10 9 8 7 6 5 4 3 2 1

ISBN (Hardcover): 978-1-95086-385-3
ISBN (eBook): 978-1-95588-470-9
LCCN: 2022914627

Cover design by Matthew Morse.
Layout design by Matthew Morse.

Since 1917, Forbes has remained steadfast in its mission to serve as the defining voice of entrepreneurial capitalism. ForbesBooks, launched in 2016 through a partnership with Advantage Media Group, furthers that aim by helping business and thought leaders bring their stories, passion, and knowledge to the forefront in custom books. Opinions expressed by ForbesBooks authors are their own. To be considered for publication, please visit **www.forbesbooks.com**.

This book is dedicated to every kid who's being counted out for going against the grain. If you've got a passion, go for it. We're living in the future—you can make a career out of anything. Don't let life tell you otherwise.

CONTENTS

PART IV: ALL THAT MATTERS IS
USING WHAT YOU'VE BUILT TO YOUR ADVANTAGE

ACKNOWLEDGMENTS

Having almost not made it out of high school, I never thought I'd be in a situation where I'd have the opportunity to write a book. For that reason, I firstly want to dedicate this book to the three most important people in my life.

To my mom, who'll never know just how much her sacrifice and love mean to me. I know I don't call home or write enough, but thank you for giving up your career to raise me. I know it was touch and go for a while, and between having to pick me up from school after being suspended or having to deal with the cops dropping me off at the front door for vandalizing a mailbox, things weren't always the easiest. But you always gave me everything I needed: the love that made it so I never had to feel what it was like to be insecure; the trust so that I always felt like someone had my back; and the support that gave me the confidence to feel like I could take over the world. I'll never receive a greater gift than having you as my mom. This book and everything it took to get to this point is for you.

To my dad, to whom I say: "I told you I had things under control."

And to my now wife, Irma. Looking back on the past ten years, I can't even imagine where I'd be if it wasn't for you. You're not just my best friend; you're also the person I admire most in this world.

Watching how you carry yourself and how you bring joy and comfort to everyone you interact with has made me a better person just by being able to watch it from afar. I don't know anybody else who would have stood directly by my side during some of my worst lows of trying to get truLOCAL off the ground. Ten years later and I still look at you the same way I did when I walked into Luxe Student Housing asking you to open the back door so I could sneak my own bed in. Who would have known it would have led to this?

This book is also for my extended family—the whole team who helped me build truLOCAL from 2016 to 2020. You all came along on this journey for your own reasons, but together we did something amazing. Some of you I knew before, and some of you I met along the way. But now and forever, regardless of where life takes us, what we accomplished at truLOCAL is something we will share forever. Without you, none of this would have been possible. I hope that you're all as proud of yourselves as I am of you. Every day—watching you grow and rise up to everything thrown your way—gave me my daily dose of inspiration. Regardless of where my own story takes me, you all have my sincere gratitude for the rest of my life. I hope to be able to have the same impact on your lives at some point as you all did on mine.

Next, I'd like to thank Chip, Laura G., Laura R., and the whole team at Forbes who helped me organize my thoughts and bring this book to life. Without you, this would all still be a notebook in Evernote. And a special thanks to Morgan McNinch—there's a good chance she's the reason you heard about this book and are reading it right now.

I'd like to also thank everybody and anybody who ever gave me a helping hand. Throughout my six years of building truLOCAL, there were more people than I could count who—without reason or incentive—have given me advice, pointed me in the right direction, opened doors, made a connection, or just lent their time my way. As a founder, sometimes we forget that it's usually a thousand small acts that make up a big success. You all know who you are. And without you, I wouldn't be here.

And last but certainly not least, I want to thank each and every single person who ever ordered a box from truLOCAL. It doesn't matter if you've been with us for 187 boxes (you know who you are), or if you ordered just once. To us, you've always been so much more than just a customer. Thank you for taking a chance on us.

Who Is This Book For, Anyway?

I figured if I'm going to write a book about what I've learned in business, I might as well set the tone right out of the gate.

If you're running a business, there's no doubt that at some point somebody made an overly smug comment about needing to find a work-life balance. You might have read it in a self-help book, heard it from a life coach, or had an overly protective friend or family member say you need to take a step back and focus more on balance. Or maybe they suggested to just take the night off because, well, "You're your own boss, aren't you?" But the hard truth is if you're the first-time founder of a start-up focusing on growth, work-life balance isn't an option.

Today, it's a hard pill to swallow, considering we're all so focused on making sure we're happy, comfortable, *and* not overworked. To emphasize the point, I'd like to take a second to time-stamp this while I'm writing. On November 9, 2021, the news section of my LinkedIn page featured five trending stories—there was one on "How to Push Back Your Start Date," and another titled "Raise a Glass to Being a Quitter." With all that being said, I did notice something that offered a bit of an answer. None of the people I saw preaching easy living or work-life balance were actually first-time founders. These stories seemed to come from people who were on their second or third profitable business, or had already accomplished what they wanted to achieve, and were perfectly content being right where they were. Being in that situation and feeling that way is fine. It's just not the mentality most first-time founders have.

Don't get me wrong—work-life balance is great. And there's nothing wrong with successful or content people preaching that we need more of it. But we need to start accepting the fact that things are different if you're a first-time founder.

So let me start off by saying that being a first-time founder is *supposed* to be hard. Think about it: you've taken on all the risk, you quit your job, and you might have convinced friends and family to join the cause. You also probably borrowed or raised some money, and now every single day is a struggle to justify all that risk.

This book is for first-time founders. Period.

All of the content in this book comes from my own personal experience. And I wrote it for a very specific group of people, so I feel like it's important to highlight who this book is for. This book is for first-time founders. Period.

A book can't be everything to all people. So I want to set the record straight before you dive in, to make sure you are totally certain *this* book is for you. At the risk of sounding too blunt, this book is for people who want to achieve great things above all else. It's for the people who, when they see someone living the life they want to live, don't get mad or jealous. Instead, their first instinct is to run up and strike a conversation with the hopes that they might learn something. There are a lot of things that I'm hoping my story can teach you, but I think one of the hardest parts for me was realizing that there is no rule book or guidebook for business. That means that nobody can tell you the right or wrong way to start a business or be successful—what we can do, however, is share stories and experiences with the hope that something resonates and maybe inspires an idea or helps solve a problem you might be facing.

With all the media, business coaches, and LinkedIn posts out there, there's no shortage of content to make you feel like there's a very specific set of rules you've got to follow if you want to be successful. It's only after you've gotten into this world that you realize that there isn't, and it's up to you to create your own guidebook and formulate your own set of rules in which you'll find your success by. I'll elaborate more later on, but one thing in particular I want to call out is believing that as a first-time founder, you can have a healthy work-life balance. If you're truly passionate about achieving what it is you're trying to achieve—your life's work—the thing you want more than anything else in this world, you'll be able to easily understand that while you're working to accomplish this "obsession" (which I consider a positive term), a work-life balance is the furthest thing from reality.

Think about it: A ball player who decided to go one-and-done after one year of college. An Olympian who has sacrificed all resemblance of a social life. An F1 driver's family who has committed every last dollar. A *Billboard* artist who dropped out of school to spend more time in the studio. A PhD student who's in year seven of a ten-year specialization. A US Navy SEAL who has given up being a civilian. In each of these situations, sacrificing *everything* to chase after a goal isn't just considered justified—it's actually *glorified*. These people sacrificed their social lives, school, friends, family, and health to dedicate every second toward their craft. But when someone decides to make the same sacrifices to build a business, we say: "You really need to find a work-life balance," or "You're working too much," or "Why are you so driven by money and success? Don't you know there's more to life?" Instead of feeling bad or thinking you're crazy or wrong, *lean into it*. You're doing something that the majority of the population can't even imagine doing. You're going on a journey that most people wouldn't be able to spend one week trying to follow. After all, you want the success that only a very small percentage of the population will ever achieve. That means you'll have to face challenges that only a very small percentage of the population will ever deal with. Never forget that your challenges will always match your ambition.

Being a first-time founder is hard. I'm not here to give you shortcuts to try and make the road easier. Instead, I'm here to share my story in the hopes that some of the tips and tricks I've learned along the way will help better prepare you and make you stronger for the road ahead. I've also been told that, when writing a book, you should spread the themes out throughout the whole book to keep readers coming back for more. I don't believe in that either, so I'm going to give you one of the main takeaways up front. Being a first-time founder is a fancy way of saying that, from here on out, your sole reason for existence is to become the best in the world at solving problems. If you plan on being a first-time founder, take special care to note "first-time." Then you need to realize that you're not a marketer or a salesperson. You're not a CEO, COO, or CTO. You're not a president or manager. As a first-time founder, you are a professional problem solver. In my experience, the faster you're able to realize that, the faster you'll be able to start adopting the right mindset in regard to your business. And as you'll find out later in the book, the right mindset is what can help you avoid burnout and power through

> **Being a first-time founder is a fancy way of saying that, from here on out, your sole reason for existence is to become the best in the world at solving problems.**

the daily (if not hourly) challenges of building a business for the first time.

I also think it's important to highlight where my experience ends. For the first five years while I was the CEO of truLOCAL, I was able to scale the company to sixty employees across Canada and the USA and up to $20 million annual recurring revenue. By doing that, there's a lot of things I learned along the way. But anything past that, there are a lot brighter and more qualified people than me to help take you on that journey beyond.

This is a business book, yes, but this is not a book for managers looking to scale their one-hundred-person team. It's not for executives looking to find that extra edge to increase their stock price. It's not for the CEO looking to take his company public. If you're at that point, congratulations; I hope to be there soon one day. But for now, this book isn't for you.

True Founder: What No One Else Has the Guts to Teach You about Starting Your First Business is for first-time founders—*all* first-time founders. If you're looking to pull the trigger and quit your job, this book is for you. If you're trying to figure out whether you should hire your first team members based on experience or take a chance on hiring friends, this book is for you. If you're trying to decide between angel funding, venture capitalist (VC) funding, or debt, this book is for you. If you're sitting there reading this, feeling like you're about to burn out and that you're doing everything wrong, this book is for you.

I've broken up the book into four parts, which follow some of the most important anecdotes, learnings, or skills that you'll need based on your progression as a first-time founder. "Part I: Set Yourself Up for Success—All That Matters Is Having the Right Mindset" is all about properly positioning yourself before you even start, to avoid a lot of the self-imposed roadblocks that most people go through when deciding to become a first-time founder. I'll go over different ways of looking at what's important when you're first getting started and give you a perspective on how to approach starting your first business. "Part II: Just Do It—All That Matters Is Getting Started" is all about just getting started. You've made the decision, and you're looking at things the right way. Now it's time to dive into some of the early challenges and milestones that come with your first year or so in business. "Part III: Horsepower—All That Matters Is Putting in the Work" is all about work. Whether it's raising money, keeping up with your skill sets and responsibilities, or growing your audience and building your community, keeping your head down and putting in the work are at the core during this stage of your journey. During this time, it's less about thinking and more about the sheer willpower to show up and do the daily tasks required to push your business forward. And finally, "Part IV: Finesse—All That Matters Is Using What You've Built to Your Advantage" is for when you've finally gotten your head above water and secured a solid foundation, and now it's time for your role to change and for you to start using a little more finesse by leveraging the resources at your disposal. This is where working on making yourself a better leader and spending more time developing your team become priority number one.

My only hope for you reading this book is that by the end, you realize it doesn't take someone special to get into business. What it takes is the right mindset, the ability to become self-aware of what makes you operate at your highest level, the dedication to put your success and goals above everything else, and, as any honest founder would say, a little bit of luck. My hope is that through reading my story and knowing how many times I almost failed, you realize that with the right attitude, a few key tips and tricks, and a little luck, you can also sell your company for $16.8 million in five years.

Also, as a quick note to end this introduction, I wanted to flag that this book wasn't actually supposed to be called *True Founder*. It was supposed to be called "truFOUNDER," playing off the lowercase "tru" of truLOCAL. I loved it, and I thought it was a great play on words, but the people over at Forbes convinced me they know a thing or two about selling books and pointed out a myriad of reasons as to why launching a book with that title would be a horrible idea. So we settled on *True Founder*. Sometimes you need to make compromises for the betterment of the business, lesson number one.

Who Am I, Anyway?

I figured I should start with why I'm qualified to write a book about what it's like to be a first-time founder. Starting from the top, my name is Marc Lafleur. Academics definitely weren't my strong suit growing up. But by putting the old saying "Cs get degrees" to the test, I managed to graduate with a Bachelor of Science, majoring in health studies from the University of Waterloo.

At twenty-two years old, I heard that Snapchat turned down a $3 billion offer to sell the company to Facebook. That's when I realized I didn't care too much about my health degree anymore. I decided to focus on business and went on to cofound an instant messaging app called Tell. That's what started it all for me.

Tell was an instant messaging platform that allowed its users to send messages that would disappear once read. Sound familiar? The thing that I was proud of, however, was the fact that we came up with the deadline feature long before anything like that had become mainstream on Snapchat or BBM. What would happen is people could set a timer, and once the message was sent, if the recipient didn't open it before the timer ran out, they would never receive it at all. We marketed it as a useful tool for planners and organizers, but we knew better. It was mostly used between the hours of 11:00 p.m. and 3:00 a.m. with deadlines set for a couple hours. I'll let you put two and two together for that one.

I had no business background, so naively I plotted on how I could build a business worth $3 billion and get the same kind of offer from Facebook. I figured if my roommates and I pooled our student loan money together, we could build an app to rival Snapchat and be millionaires by the summer. Needless to say, that's not what happened.

Six months after launch, I accidentally deleted all our users. I have a full talk that I've given on the topic that you can find on my website, but needless to say that was the end of my first start-up.

Tell was a great trial by fire into the business world. Without that experience, nothing that followed would ever have happened, so I'm the proudest of that failure. Believe it or not, even after Tell failed, I realized I really wanted to do it again. I took what I learned from getting Tell off the ground, partnered with a computer science student from the University of Waterloo, and built a website that let students do random tasks and odd jobs for cash, called DashTask.

In 2014, I was inspired by the buzz around the *sharing economy*. Companies were popping up that leveraged the idea of sharing resources for the betterment of the community. With companies like TaskRabbit paving the way, I figured there would be a way to leverage a proven business model but launch it in a niche market. With DashTask, students could earn extra cash by doing random tasks that were posted by other students on campus. Busy students could save time by posting things like: "I need someone to do my laundry," or "I need someone to grab my groceries." We made it further than we did with Tell, but then my cofounder got recruited by Google, and I couldn't get any funding. So DashTask joined Tell on my growing tally of hard life lessons.

I was on a roll—two failed start-ups by the age of twenty-five.

After Tell and DashTask, I ended up really putting my degree to work by getting a job as a door-to-door meat salesman. It paid surprisingly well. I realized that people loved the product, but the business model made no sense. I had actually worked my way up to becoming the top sales rep in the company, eventually earning the opportunity to come off the road and open my own office. I was twenty-five years old and personally making over $200,000 a year. I actually suggested to the owners of the company that they take the model online, but they literally laughed me out of the room. A few months later, my cofounder at truLOCAL, Greg, and I quit to do it on our own. We decided that we could take best practices from the e-commerce world and bring it to small producers, helping them connect with their customers at a larger scale. That's how truLOCAL was born.

Founded in February 2016, truLOCAL became an online marketplace that let people order products from local butchers, producers, and suppliers in their area. People could go online and mix and match hundreds of different meat cuts into their own customized box and have it delivered to their front door every month. In 2016, companies were still struggling to not only figure out how to ship meat and keep it frozen but also how to get customers to open their minds to ordering frozen meat in the mail.

Over the course of five years—as cofounder and CEO of truLOCAL—the team grew to over sixty employees and expanded across the country. I was fortunate to represent the team and company on the cover of *The Globe and Mail's* Report on Business for being Canada's fourteenth top growing company during that time. We accumulated a series of wins, including a successful pitch on *Dragons' Den* in 2017, well on our way to becoming the country's largest D2C (direct to consumer) protein business, culminating with a $16.8 million acquisition in 2020.

After my time at truLOCAL I got into angel investing, partly to see if I could develop a knack for choosing winning businesses, and partly because I genuinely enjoy spending time with up-and-coming founders. Not only do I get to share my knowledge and expertise with them, but they always make sure I stay sharp as well.

Even though I had a hate-hate relationship with academia, I did find myself somewhat interested in formalized business training. I was fortunate enough to be accepted into the Directors Education Program (DEP) of the Institute of Corporate Directors and have recently become one of the youngest graduates from DEP91 in October 2021. The Director Education Program put on by the institute of corporate directors is a globally renowned, executive-level education program focused on expanding the skillsets and knowledge base of already seasoned directors so that they can become even more effective in the board room.

And lastly but still noteworthy, in addition to being able to share my thoughts on entrepreneurship privately to my clients and founders I've invested in, I've also been sharing these learnings through public speaking for companies and institutions like Lululemon, Google, and FedEx, as well as at academic institutions like the University of Waterloo and keynote talks at various conferences across Canada and the United States.

Still, as you'll soon find out, I find it crazy to write about myself in this way because, at the end of the day, I'm just "Dark Marc." The kid with the messy afro who wasn't even supposed to graduate high school. All this to say that it got to the point where I realized that my life experiences have become fairly unique to a thirty-year-old, and I want to put my perspective into the world in the hopes that it might help or inspire someone on their own journey.

PART I

All That Matters Is Having the Right Mindset

CHAPTER ONE

Becoming a Professional Problem Solver

Don't fight in the North or the South. Fight every battle everywhere, always, in your mind. Everyone is your enemy; everyone is your friend.

Every possible series of events is happening all at once. Live that way and nothing will surprise you. Everything that happens will be something that you've seen before.

—LITTLEFINGER, GAME OF THRONES

Like I mentioned in the introduction, out of all the skills you can learn as a first-time founder, there's one that stands out above the rest. You're going to have punches thrown at your head each and every single day. It doesn't matter how well you can code, create great content, or close deals. If you can't problem solve at a high level, you're not going to make it.

A lot of people talk about what it means to be a first-time founder. But I'm here to break it down to *one* thing that you can always remember: You're not a CEO, CMO, or CTO. You're not a head of sales or a president. As a first-time founder, you are a professional problem solver. The sooner you realize this fact, the more confidence you'll have and the less stressful your mornings will be. The more you'll lean into who you are and what you're good at as a first-time founder. And the quicker you'll be able to react when something inevitably goes wrong.

Things are always obvious in retrospect. Looking back on what mattered in the early days is very different once you've had time to reflect with a clear mind. It's easy to see what mattered, what helped, and what you would do differently. But looking at it when you're just starting off and embracing your journey as a first-time founder, it can be hard to anticipate what's going to help you along the way and what's going to be a waste of time. The biggest piece of advice I'd give myself looking back is that in the early days, you don't have time to think a month or a quarter ahead. These early days are your most important and most formative. These early days are about survival.

You need to deal with the problems that are showing up on a day-to-day basis. That was my mistake—I always wanted to brush up on skills that I thought would help me in the future. Like most people, I wanted to cherry-pick what I focused on and spend most of my time on the things that I thought were cool or interesting. But what I didn't realize back then was that if I didn't focus on solving the problems that were right in front of me, I'd never make it to a point where I'd be able to work on the so-called "cool" or "interesting" problems.

It's not glamorous, but working on becoming a professional problem solver is effective and the most efficient use of your time. You need to learn that things never get easier in business. We have this idea that once you hire your first employee, or once you raise your first round of funding, things will get easier. But that's not the case. You might have a day or even a week of relief, but soon you'll realize the problems are still there—they're just bigger. Starting a business by definition means you need to continuously solve problems. Ideally, your business is either improving on something that already exists or providing something that doesn't exist yet—inherently trying to do either of those things mean you're venturing into unknown territory and going to be dealing with problems head-on.

Understanding that your problems are never going to go away will not only help you deal with these problems in a systematic way, which we'll touch on shortly, but it will also help reduce stress. I remember the days where I'd wake up, and as soon as I realized that I was awake, I'd immediately feel that shot of cortisol race through my veins. If you've been in that situation before, you know exactly what I'm talking about. It's hard to describe because it doesn't hurt, but at the same time it's like ice and fire just got injected down your spine. The hair on the back of my neck would stand up, and I'd immediately start searching my mind for answers as to why I would ever pursue anything that ever made me feel this way. I just wanted to roll over and go back to sleep. This was a daily ritual in my first year, and probably one that most first-time founders go through. It was hard, and it was sad, but what other option did I have? I was a first-time founder. It was either win or go bust.

There were a lot of times where I was "playing" founder rather than actually being one.

It took getting to the finish line and finally getting acquired to realize what really served me well. There were a lot of times where I was "playing" founder rather than actually being one. And one of the things that stood out the most were the skills I would focus on developing. I remember when I went down the data-analytics rabbit hole. I'd spend hours on LinkedIn, following whichever LinkedIn expert was relevant at the time to learn how to properly incorporate a strong data infrastructure at truLOCAL. This was hilarious, because at the time the business consisted of myself and my business partner, Greg. Why the hell was I spending my days learning about advanced data warehousing and how to properly standardize data between departments? It definitely wasn't helping me deal with the day-to-day issues we were having. It didn't help me deal with the fact that we were packing customer orders off Excel spreadsheets, which led to boxes being packed incorrectly, which led to a mountain of customer service issues. And it definitely didn't help us develop new value propositions to deal with the wave of copycat competitors popping up on a weekly basis in our main markets.

I remember other times where I'd spend my days on the phone with our couriers trying to get an understanding as to why a couple hundred of our perishable packages didn't leave their sorting facilities on time, only to find out that the dangerous goods labels we had printed on our boxes were the wrong color. To keep our products frozen while they were in transit, we used dry ice. This worked really well, except for the fact that shipping companies consider dry ice as a dangerous good, which means we had to have special labels on our boxes indicating the fact that there was dry ice inside. Usually these labels are stickers that you have to manually slap on each box. We got crafty and decided to just print our boxes with the label design already in place to save time. But seeing as our boxes were black, the labels printed onto our boxes came out black and white, rather than white and black. This mess up led to a few thousand dollars of our products going to waste. And, of course, a mountain of emails from customers canceling, threatening bad reviews, or just letting us know in general how disappointed they were.

It wasn't until about a year into the business that I started realizing there didn't seem to be any rhyme or reason for the problems that popped up. They didn't seem to discriminate based on time, discipline, department, scope, or theme. They just happened. But I also noticed that, over time, we'd gotten pretty good at dodging those bullets. Eventually, after a prolonged bombardment of daily issues, I just started anticipating it. It went from *I hope we don't have any issues today* to *I wonder if I'll make it to noon without having to put out a fire.* It went from hearing about a problem and having my whole world come crashing down around me and wondering how I was going to pull the energy to even diagnose the issue, let alone put a solution together, to hearing about a problem and it immediately triggering this muscle memory reaction of survey, triage, and execute.

It's easy to say while looking back, and I'm sure the version of me that was living through this time would hate me for saying this, but it almost got to the point where I was excited when I'd hear about a problem (when people say you need to be a little psychotic to be a founder, that's the part they're talking about!). All it took was swallowing the truth that I was never going to reach a point where problems didn't stop coming. That revelation led me to adopt a mindset of anticipation.

That was a real turning point for me. Anticipating problems made my mornings better, because instead of waking up and praying that I didn't have a ten-ton megabomb of an email sitting in my inbox, I'd wake up knowing that there was. And for me, just accepting on a daily basis that was what I was going to have to deal with saved me a lot of unnecessary stress.

I'll never forget the first time I received an email from our old company threatening to sue us. When you're a first-time founder and have never dealt with another business legally before, waking up to an email like that is almost enough to make you want to throw up, shut down, and go back to bed until next month. That's what it was like dealing with problems in the early days, where I was just hoping for things to get easier. Contrast that to about a year later when we had been through a couple battles and finally became pretty good problem solvers. I woke up one day to an email from a buddy showing me an ex-employee who had literally copied our entire website. Not just the business model but all the way down to the pictures, descriptions, and FAQs. Trust me, that's a really shitty feeling as well, but the difference between this morning and the morning when I woke up to that email from our old company was, that particular morning, I was already expecting a problem to deal with.

Anticipating problems made my reaction time better and, therefore, the time it took to solve a problem significantly shorter. Anytime you're prepared for something, you're going to be able to react faster. If you've just dodged a bullet, solved a problem, and had a major accomplishment, and you're now hoping that's the last of it and that nothing bad is going to happen anymore, how are you going to react when that bad thing inevitably does happen? You'll start with depression, probably go through a little bit of denial. And if you're in a really dark place, you'll probably avoid it altogether before getting your shit together and starting to tackle the issue.

Whereas if you're *always* anticipating, waiting for that problem, knowing it's a few minutes, hours, or days away from coming, when it does come, you're ready. You'll lean into it, and you'll immediately triage the issue—which means you'll come up with a game plan significantly quicker. And if you really lean into sharpening your iron as a professional problem solver, you'll get to a point where anticipating problems means that subconsciously you'll start gaming out scenarios to problems that don't even exist—yet. Which means that when those problems do pop up, you might already have an answer to it without even having to spend the time or resources dealing with it.

So how do you actually become a professional problem solver? Well, if I had to break down my process into words, it would be this:

SURVEY → TRIAGE → EXECUTE

Survey the problem, triage your best options, execute your solution, and, most importantly, understand that there is always a way out. Always.

Survey

Once you understand that there's always a way out, you can start tackling the issue. Start by taking stock of your resources. Is it just you? Do you have a cofounder or team you can lean on if you need to? If you're fortunate enough to have a cofounder or a team, make sure to tap them in. As a professional problem solver and a first-time founder, your job is to leverage all assets, and your team is your *best* asset. So if you've got a team or a partner, make sure that you're using their problem-solving abilities to amplify your own.

Once you've taken stock of your resources and you know how much or how little you have to work with, survey the problem. Does this problem require time, money, or finesse? Maybe all three? Is your problem one that can be solved in one step? Or is it a problem that needs to be solved in multiple steps? If you're a visual person, literally write this out. If you can game out the entirety of the problem and try to solve all of it in one go, do that. But personally, I've found this to be pretty hard, and you need to be pretty lucky to come up with one solution for the whole problem. Most problems seem to be broken down into parts, which require you to solve them in multiple steps. If you survey that there are three parts to a particular problem, depending on how you deal with the first part, it may open or close doors to the second and third parts of the problem. So instead of making assumptions on how to deal with parts two and three, start by just dealing with the first part of the problem. Once you have an answer for that, you can narrow down and focus your options for step two, then apply the same process to step three.

Now that you've got a good understanding of the problem, it's time to start listing out solutions. At this point in the process, it doesn't matter if they are good ideas or bad ideas; just list them all out. I can't stress this enough, even if the solutions don't make sense. As long as they're doable, make sure they're on the list.

Triage

By triaging your list of solutions, this is where you'll figure out what solution is either the best or the *least worst* for your problem. Some problems let you generate a long list of solutions; other problems leave you with fewer viable solutions, or sometimes even just one. But one thing I will promise is that it may not be an ideal solution, but you'll always have at least one.

At this point, you've listed out all possible solutions, and now it's time to run a process of elimination. Start scratching out the ideas that are not viable due to cost/expenses, legal risk/reputational risk, resources, or operational limitations. If you've turned over every stone and tapped into all resources (and I mean *all*—make sure you're also thinking outside the box), in a perfect world, you'll be left with one optimal option. But don't forget, optimal can still mean less than ideal or, in some cases, overall bad, and that's okay. Solutions to problems are meant to be better than letting the problem run wild. It doesn't always mean it's an ideal solution. It just needs to be better than the issue at hand. I can remember a number of times where I'd have to say: "Look, we're in a critical situation; this isn't supposed to be easy or fun. These solutions both suck, but they're better than what we're dealing with right now."

Execute

This is the simplest step in the process. But with that being said, simple doesn't always mean easy. At this point you have your solution, and your job is to now start executing against it to solve your problem.

Having the mindset of a professional problem solver isn't easy. I find myself constantly needing to remind myself why I'm a problem solver. And I have kept that mindset sharp, especially in the later years of truLOCAL right before our acquisition, where I felt like I had built up a team and resources that would help shield myself and the business from the major existential threats. But, of course, it was in those moments of weakness when all sorts of problems somehow found cracks in the armor.

An example of this was dealing with our refrigeration units. As the universe would have it, for some reason our refrigeration units always seemed to decide to break down on long weekends. I wish I had an explanation for it; these units typically only require a yearly inspection or servicing but tend to be pretty hands off and reliable otherwise. But this recurring problem was like clockwork. If there was a long weekend, our freezers would go out. As a company that sells frozen food, you can imagine how bad this can be.

> Solutions to problems are meant to be better than letting the problem run wild. It doesn't always mean it's an ideal solution.

For those of you who don't know, when you're dealing with industrial freezers, you've got a small window of time for how long the area will stay below 0°C once you have a failure. What I can confidently say is that it's not a long weekend's worth of time. And because this issue happened on a long weekend (a.k.a. a holiday weekend), no repair companies were available to deal with emergencies.

I'll never forget when this happened on the Saturday night of a Canada Day long weekend. My now wife, but at the time girlfriend of five years, Irma, and I were getting ready for bed. After about a year of building truLOCAL with just Greg and myself, we decided that we needed someone else that we trusted to help us with the day-to-day. Because we lived together, Irma saw the ins and outs of what we were going through to grow truLOCAL, and she was already helping me problem solve on a regular basis, so she became truLOCAL's first employee.

It was around 11:00 p.m., and after a couple years of trying to build truLOCAL, 11:00 p.m. might as well have been 3:00 a.m. to us. There was nothing that we cared more about on our weekends than just shutting down early and getting some good sleep so we could recover for the upcoming week.

The notice came to my phone first. After a refrigeration unit scare the previous year, we installed monitoring systems in the freezers, and they were showing the temperature rising. This was our first stroke of luck and an example of anticipating problems before they happen. We didn't even know exactly what the issue was, but we just knew there was a freezer issue, partly because of the fact the temperature was rising but also because of the simple fact it was a long weekend. You can probably assume, but neither of us are technicians. Nor do we know anything about freezers outside of how to turn them on. Our warehouse at the time had two industrial-sized freezers, each of which probably contained about a hundred fifty-pound boxes of frozen meat. We didn't know what to do. But we did know we had to get our asses down to the warehouse ASAP to see what was going on.

When we arrived, we immediately started surveying the problem. One of the two freezers had iced up and wasn't circulating air because it was stuffed so full of meat. Every so often as a regular maintenance task, we needed to de-ice them, which obviously we had failed to do on time. Now there was a five-inch-thick wall of ice clogging up the back where the air was supposed to blow, putting stress on the compressor. With our problem understood and surveyed, we jumped into triage mode. We called suppliers to find a refrigeration truck. We called every freezer rental company in the area. No luck.

Realizing we had zero outside help, we had to figure out a solution ourselves. Ultimately, we decided we needed to move the boxes over to the other freezer. Sounds simple enough. But remember, we're talking about me and Irma moving over a hundred fifty-pound boxes by ourselves.

Honestly, it's hard to put in words, but just assume it was brutal. Plus, it was now 2:00 a.m. After hours of breaking our backs, we noticed that the good freezer was now losing proper circulation because it was getting too full as well. We started panicking that we were suddenly going to lose both freezers! We didn't know if the other freezer's compressor was broken or not, but we decided to chip away at the ice and try to get air circulating again either way. Now, I've got to explain something here: this ice isn't cute, little fragile pieces of ice. This is thick, frozen blocks of ice melded onto metal. It took some serious effort and digging to get this chipped away. It got to the point where we eventually needed to use a blowtorch and a crowbar. But it started working. The first freezer began getting airflow again, and the temp was dropping. That's when we went back to hauling boxes, refilling the first freezer with what we had removed just hours earlier.

This is just one small example, but things like this are what it's like to be a first-time founder and professional problem solver. There isn't a formula or equation to follow. It's not a specific skill you can learn. It's just a mental toughness you need to face the problem and realize nobody else is going to save you. You either solve the problem, or you fail.

There's a lot of pressure that comes with being a first-time founder, but the sooner you realize your role is to be a professional problem solver, the sooner you'll become a more effective leader.

CHAPTER TWO

Business Is a Series of Sprints, Not a Marathon

There's a reason the last man standing is usually the winner.

—JORDAN COLEMAN

I always hated that saying: "Business is a marathon, not a sprint." I can confidently tell you that, regardless of whether you look at it as a marathon or a sprint, the only thing in common is: Exhaustion.

With that being said, after going through a few different stages of growth, I really started to realize that there's a cyclical nature to running a business. The best way I can describe it is to say there's a cadence. You seem to always either be in an all-or-nothing dash for some sort of major milestone, like a product launch, or closing a financing round, *or* you are dedicating all your time toward obsessing over the systems and process of your business, trying to squeeze that last percent out of your margin, or streamlining communication between departments to make things more efficient. It almost becomes predictable. Once I started to understand that, I started to notice some subtle differences between treating business like a marathon versus treating it like a series of sprints.

I get the analogy that MBAs and business professors are trying to make with comparing business to a marathon. At first glance it makes sense. Business is long, and marathons are long. "Save your energy" and "Make sure you don't burn out too soon" are common comparisons. They use phrases like *slow and steady wins the race* and *you're in it for the long haul*. These all make sense and definitely have their place in business—but not when you're a first-time founder.

You've probably heard it before, and it's the truth. As a first-time founder, you're at war. And if you're the soldier on the battlefield who's thinking, "Hmmm, I probably should save my energy for the next battle," you probably won't make it to the next battle. So let's look at this: saving your energy, playing it safe, thinking about "slow and steady" is exactly how you'd run your business if you compared it to a marathon. But how does that actually translate? As a marathon-running, first-time founder, while you are calmly and coolly making a decision and moving toward that decision at the same energy-saving pace as you would if you were running a marathon, your competitors—with a different mindset—might be sprinting toward that metaphorical water station at the next checkpoint. And unlike in a marathon, in business, there's not enough water for everyone.

The issue with approaching business in the same way that you'd approach a marathon is two-fold: (1) you'll be beat every time by a founder who's sprinting toward the same milestone; and (2) due to constant sustained exertion, you're actually more likely to burn out due to lack of rest or recovery.

In business, you never know when your finish line might come. Imagine you're in the last ten minutes of a four hour marathon. Your whole game plan is based around making sure you can last those four hours, and that you have enough energy to make it through the entire race. Now imagine if three-and-a-half hours in, you got an email to your smart watch saying that due to circumstances completely outside of your control, they, for some reason, decided to extend the race by another hour. Physically, you'd have absolutely zero gas left in the tank. And mentally you'd probably crack—break down and cry. You played your strategy to perfection, but the rules of the game changed. Not dissimilar at all from life as a first-time founder. As marathons go, you never had a chance to rest or recharge. And now, because you've been slowly and consistently draining your tank, in your weakened and vulnerable state, you can't continue.

This is the reality for most businesses. Right when you think you've made it, a problem comes up that pushes out the finish line. Because you've never had a chance to rest or refill your tanks, because you never had the chance to celebrate some sort of win or victory, you and your company end up taking sustained abuse over time that will ultimately cause it to collapse. Eventually you will burn out. And while you are focusing on maintaining your slow and steady pace, the competition took a different approach.

> A first-time founder's ability to adapt is what's going to keep them alive. But speed is what will make them successful.

Now, let's take a look at what would happen if you looked at business from a sprinter's mindset. Sprints are short, targeted bursts of energy and focus toward the finish line. And when short periods of rest and recovery are placed between sprints, the runner can string successful sprints together—or, when applied to business, string together consecutive wins.

With this model in mind, let's look at being a sprinting, first-time founder. As referenced above, a first-time founder's ability to adapt is what's going to keep them alive. But speed is what will make them successful. Let's say you're in heated negotiations with a VC or angel investor who is looking to invest in your space, and they've point-blank told you that they're down to the wire and are now trying to decide between you and another company. Would you decide to not follow up, or put those extra hours in on your pitch deck because you don't want to use too much energy? Are you going to play it safe and let them reach back out to you? Of course not. You are going to be laser-focused. You are going to push everything else to the wayside. You're going to reprioritize all your available resources toward this massive opportunity. You're going to take all the risks you need to get ahead and beat your competition to the finish line.

SPRINTER

SHORT WINS

END IN SIGHT

HIGH OFF ACCOMPLISHMENT

MARATHONER

HARD TO STAY MOTIVATED

DEPLETING ENERGY

NO RECOVERY

Being a first-time founder means sprinting toward that next major client. It means sprinting toward launching or getting your product to market. It means sprinting toward your next raise. These are just examples of some of the milestones you are or will be facing. And to win as a first-time founder, it's not only required that you use all of your available energy and focus toward going after these goals, but it's also *okay* to use all of your energy and focus on going after these goals. If the opportunity is big enough, like a sprinter, it's okay to use up everything you have in the tank to make it a reality.

But with all this being said, comparing business to being a sprinter doesn't put the whole picture together either. If you want to treat business like a series of sprints, you can only get away with that if you recognize one more important concept. You can't just sprint and sprint and sprint and sprint and sprint. Otherwise, you'll also fade away like the first-time founder running an endless marathon. Treating business like a series of sprints is just that—a *series* of sprints. This means you have time *in between sprints*, and this time in between sprints is arguably the most important part. That's where the cyclical nature of a business comes in. If you want to have a series of sprints, you need a recovery period.

> If the opportunity is big enough, like a sprinter, it's okay to use up everything you have in the tank to make it a reality.

There are a lot of different examples that you can use when it comes to sprinting toward a milestone. But what happens is, once you raise that money or close that client, or once you launch that product, there might not be a direct sprint or a new milestone right in front of you. Right away, there might not even be another opportunity in front of you.

The reality is that when you sprint toward something, it comes at a cost. It's not only the mental energy, but maybe you sacrifice margins, maybe you sacrifice quality and process, maybe you launch imperfect products. You make promises that you can't keep as a salesperson trying to get these milestones. So you eventually need to take a step back and say, "Okay, we did what we set out to do. Now let's fix all the stuff that we've broken along the way." For sprinters, this is your recovery period. For first-time founders, this is where you recharge, optimize, and prioritize. I'd break down the steps to taking full advantage of your recovery period like this:

Recharge

This phase is done exactly how it sounds. You and your team need to rest. You'll never escape the long nights and early mornings as a first-time founder, but you do need some self-care after a big win. And in this phase, you do whatever it is that you do to get that care. This is where you take a breath and check the morale of the team. It's the recharge phase between sprints that helps you avoid burnouts and spinouts. But that doesn't mean you're on vacation. The recharge period doesn't mean you take your mind off the game.

> It's the recharge phase between sprints that helps you avoid burnouts and spinouts.

Optimize

When there are no other immediate opportunities right in front of you, you're going to go back and do a postmortem check on what just happened during your sprint: the good, the bad, and the ugly. Remember how I said that you'd throw everything to the wayside to focus on the goal right in front of you? Well, those things you threw to the wayside now need attention. Margins are a really good example of something that suffers while you sprint toward a goal. If you needed to sprint toward a certain revenue target to impress your investors, there's a good chance you offered promotions or discounts on your product to help boost revenues. You probably also did it to the point where your margins are no longer sustainable. It is during this optimize phase where you'll decide if returning to your original price and marketing strategy is the way to go, or if optimizing your purchasing and inventory management system to maintain your margins is a smarter move.

The communication channel between your team and throughout your business is also a good example, and one that I'll always remember from truLOCAL. During the pandemic, we had to do some major sprinting to hire enough staff to deal with the increase in demand. We went from an $8 million run rate to a $20 million run rate, and a thirty-member team to a team of more than sixty in just six weeks. We beefed up (no pun intended) all of our departments, which was great. But what we didn't improve at the same scale was our communication strategy within the team, nor how different departments communicated and collaborated with one another. You get to a certain point where you reach diminishing returns, and more people doesn't mean more productivity. For us, having a sprinter's focus on hiring is what allowed us to stay open all through the pandemic. But taking the time to optimize how our team communicated via Slack, email, Asana, and Jira is what allowed us to stay efficient and keep operating well at the new size.

Prioritize

Finally, more likely than not after a sprint, your business has changed dramatically, which can mean that the things that were important before you got the win are different from the things that are important *after* the win. Use this recovery period to draft up a new road map. This is the calm before the next storm, and using this time to plan out your new priorities is what will help prevent you from potentially sprinting toward the wrong opportunities moving forward. I've found that looking at your business after the sprint as though it's a completely new business does a really good job in helping prioritize what's important next, or which opportunities are most accessible.

Depending on what milestone you just achieved, take a second to look at your newly loaded business and ask, "If I were starting this business again today with all the resources I have now, what would I do? Where would I start? How would it look?" When you started your business, it was just you and maybe a cofounder. You had no money, no experience, no product, and no network. As a professional problem solver, you mapped out in your head how you'd be successful with the limited resources you had. Well, fast-forward to where you are now. How would you approach starting your business if you had all the resources currently at your disposal?

> Looking at your business after the sprint as though it's a completely new business does a really good job in helping prioritize what's important next.

You probably have a small team, maybe a little money in the bank, and some loyal customers. I bet your priorities and what you'd go after would probably be a little different. After your business has upgraded from your sprint, make sure you upgrade your point of view as well.

Being a first-time founder for the long haul is always going to be hard, but that doesn't mean you can't strategically take your foot off the gas a little in order to rebalance the car, so that when you put your foot back down, you go a lot farther, a lot faster. While you're in your recharge, optimize, and prioritize phase, have a meeting with your partner or key team members. Do a full assessment of what's working well and what could use an overhaul. Are there any recurring issues that are preventing you or your team from being efficient? Leaning into the "it's a series" part of treating business like a series of sprints is what will give you as a first-time founder a competitive mindset over everybody else following the crowd.

CHAPTER THREE

Your Job Is to Make Decisions, Even if They Aren't the Right Ones

When a bad idea is the only idea, it becomes the greatest idea.

—ADAM REED

I've said how problem-solving is the single most important skill you can develop as a first-time founder. But I've found that sometimes people don't give as much thought to *decision-making*. The difference is this:

Problem-solving is your ability to reason through an issue and find the best possible way out of a crisis or bad situation.

Decision-making is having the ability and confidence to call the shots, accept the plan, and take responsibility for whatever the outcome may be.

There are a lot of different ways to talk about decision-making. But there's one aspect of decision-making that's unique to first-time founders, and I want to make sure to touch on it early on: decision-making as a first-time founder isn't about getting every decision right. That's like thinking the fate of your business rests on every single decision. Even though certain decisions may carry that kind of weight, thinking that every choice you make is do or die is going to take you down a dark path that will more likely than not lead to decision paralysis from analyzing too many different options—or particularly for first-time founders, getting anxious about pulling the trigger on important decisions.

ANY DECISION
IS BETTER THAN
NO DECISION

PROBLEM SOLVING	DECISION MAKING
SURVEYING THE PROBLEM	MAKING A JUDGEMENT CALL
TRIAGING SOLUTIONS	CHOOSING AN OPTION
EXECUTING THE PLAN	STANDING BEHIND DECISIONS

It's obvious it would be great to be right more often than wrong. Almost by default, if you had a winning percentage that skews toward being right, you're almost guaranteed some semblance of success. But I think there's a better way to frame decision-making and give you more control over your decisions, rather than just hoping you're going to make the right calls. Instead of focusing on getting every decision right every time, start understanding that as a first-time founder, your job is to make decisions. *Period.* And if you make the wrong decision, it's your job to put the extra work in to turn it into the right decision. For the sake of productivity, for the sake of your team, for the preservation of momentum, to avoid decision paralysis, and to fulfill your responsibility as the leader of your business, your job is to make the call and stand by it.

To be efficient, you need to make decisions. Notice I didn't use any qualifiers there. I didn't say you need to be able to make the *right* decision. I didn't say you need to be able to make the *perfect* decision. You just need to be able to make *a* decision. That means being able to make a decision, then regardless of the outcome being adaptable enough to dial in adjustments along the way to get you back on track toward your goals.

The reality is that most of the time when you make a wrong decision, it doesn't mean the end of the world. Look at it like this: before you make your decision, you're starting at zero. The goal of this game is just to get to ten. Let's say, scenario 1, you choose the right decision. By making the right choice, you've given yourself an advantage, and just based on that right decision alone, you'll be starting your game at four or five on your way to getting to ten. Now let's look at scenario 2, where you make the wrong decision. Most people think if you make the wrong decision, the game is completely over; you give up. You're not even trying to get to ten anymore. But the reality is instead of making the right decision and starting at a four or a five, all you've done by making the wrong decision is now you're starting the game at negative one.

You're still in the game. You just need to accept that you now start in a less advantageous position. You'll just have to work a little harder or a little smarter to get back to break even. Yes, it will take more time, energy, and resources to work your way from your negative one all the way up to the positive four or five you would have started at if you made the right decision, but at least you can get started. A majority of the time when you make a bad decision, all that happens is you start with less of an advantage; it's not always a total loss. Going into decision-making with the mindset that most of your poor decisions can be fixed or overcome with putting in the extra work can help you avoid becoming gun shy and help give you the confidence you need to make decisions and keep the ball rolling.

> You're better off making wrong decisions with the mentality that hard work can get you out of them than not making decisions at all and stagnating your business.

You're better off making wrong decisions with the mentality that hard work can get you out of them than not making decisions at all and stagnating your business. This is because just the act of making the wrong decision means you've at least practiced the skill of decision-making, which is beneficial and should become a habit. From there, making the wrong decision and having to work your way out of it means that you're becoming a better problem solver.

Experience is so important, and even though making the wrong decision sounds bad, you're getting more opportunities to practice problem-solving, which in turn helps you discover more ways to deal with the issues that will inevitably pop up later in your journey. If you only made the right decisions or no decisions at all in the early days, how are you supposed to be prepared when the big problems start popping up? And lastly, making a decision, even if it's the wrong one, helps avoid procrastination, which is a silent killer for many first-time founders. Needless to say, these are all perspectives that should help you become more comfortable with decision-making.

I've got to drill this one home, because as someone who's decided to start a business for the first time, your job in the short term is to get and keep the ball rolling. It's to pull the trigger and incrementally move forward each and every day. The way to achieve this is with forward momentum, and forward momentum is a product of rapid decision-making.

> **Your job in the short term is to get and keep the ball rolling. It's to pull the trigger and incrementally move forward each and every day.**

I want to pause here because, yes, it's good to become comfortable with making the wrong decisions so that you can be better at decision-making in general. But there is a right way and a wrong way to do this. In this case, let's not jump to the extremes. Some aspects of business require balance and finesse, and this is one of them. I'm not saying dive headlong into saying *yea* or *nay* on things just for the sake of it. When you have the luxury of time and resources, take full advantage of all your problem-solving steps, gather as much information as possible to make an educated decision, tap into all of your resources in a timely manner, and see if you can come out with the best probable outcome. But sometimes, time and resources are a luxury that you don't have every time you're faced with a decision to make. So what do you do when you're in this sort of situation?

This is where you need to start realizing the two important factors of decision-making, time and information:

- Time: the amount of time you have before you're required to make the decision
- Information: the amount of detail, insight, perspective, context, and facts that you're able to gather about the situation

In a perfect world, you'll have as much time as you'd like to make decisions. It's funny, because you start realizing that if time wasn't an option, almost all decisions become pretty easy to deal with. Now think about it the other way: almost all decisions become exponentially more difficult as soon as there's a ticking clock behind you. Simple decisions can become complex and difficult when you're under a time crunch. The reason for this is because now you're limited in how much information you can gather.

If I want to make a good decision, I gather as much information as possible from as many sources as possible for as long as I can. Information is king, and if you can gather all possible pieces of information, your decision-making process becomes a lot easier. But in the real world where we tend to spend most of our time, the decisions we need to make are time-sensitive. In which case, now you need to weigh the pros and cons. What's the more important factor in this decision: time or information?

Very often you'll realize that *time* is the limiting factor. Maybe you need to pull the trigger on purchasing inventory on sale, but you need to let your vendor know in the next twenty-four hours or you'll lose out on the deal, meaning that you won't make your margins for this month. Or maybe you just had an amazing job interview with a candidate who's absolutely perfect, but they want 10 percent more than you were willing to offer, and you know if you don't send the offer by the end of the day, they'll accept a job elsewhere. These are examples of decisions where you'll be forced to make a choice with limited information because time is the factor.

Not making a decision makes you more likely to miss out on opportunities, and it also shows a lack of leadership to your team. If we actually played out this example, it would probably look something like this:

You'd start by gathering all the information possible in the time allowed, which isn't much. You don't have time to check references, so you go on LinkedIn to see if there are any recommendations. Maybe you check to see if you have mutual connections or someone in your network you could fire a message off to. You quickly bring up your forecast and see if your budget allows for the extra spend and realize it doesn't, so you immediately call a meeting with your team or your cofounder to see if you can shave off some additional expenses to make it work. You realize there were a couple service subscriptions, a print campaign, and the nice-to-have-but-not-necessary trade show banner that could be cut. That means if you absolutely needed to carve out the additional budget to take a chance on this individual, you could. Also, seeing as you've decided to include your cofounder or whole team, you're getting information you wouldn't have thought of on your own, and someone out of left field says, "Are there any grants available for this?" You don't have time to apply for a grant, but a quick Google search does in fact show that there is a grant you could potentially qualify for to help recruit talent. While still not perfect, and despite it being much more beneficial to have extra time, you've now gathered as much information as you can before the EOD. It's time to make your decision.

Scenario A: You hire this individual, and it works out. This is the easy answer. You collected your information, you took an educated chance, and it paid off. Congratulations. Your ability to make a decision under pressure has paid off.

Scenario B: Now the outcome you've been afraid of—you hire this individual, and it doesn't work out. Having an employee not work out can be one of the costliest mistakes you make in your business. But let's just take a second to actually look at what's happened. You're three months into having this individual, and you decide to part ways. Yes, you've wasted time, money, and resources on hiring and training this person just to have to start all over again. You're now in a position where you're at negative one rather than positive five. But you know that by working smart and hard, you can turn this into a win.

Right off the bat, you're going to do a postmortem check on what happened. Was it the hiring process? Was it the rush to make a decision? Was it the way the individual was screened? Was it the questions that were asked during the interview? Regardless of what exactly went wrong, you and your team decide to improve your current hiring process to reduce or avoid the chances of making a bad hire again in the future. Seeing as you're in this for the long haul, no doubt making this mistake early on and the subsequent changes, even if minor, will help save you from making this mistake again. You made a mistake, but now you have a better process to show for it. During your information-gathering process, you also realized that there were a couple wasted dollars floating around, so you also had a minor win there. And finally, the grant. If you weren't committed to making a decision and therefore dig for as much information as possible, you never would have known about this grant that can and will help you for future hires as well.

Decision-making isn't supposed to be easy, but you can make it simpler by setting up principles or systems to help you with your decision-making. A great book on setting up principles for life is *Principles* by Ray Dalio, which I highly recommend if you want to become less emotional and more strategic with your decision-making.

These are just scenarios, and you can play them out in a million and one different ways as long as you understand that, at the end of the day, it's all about gaining the confidence to make decisions and avoid stalling your business—even if they're the wrong ones. Not making a decision makes you more likely to miss out on opportunities, and it also shows a lack of leadership to your team. Through intuition and experience, you'll start to realize that you're making better decisions more consistently. And that's what will help you move faster than your competition.

CHAPTER FOUR

How to Stay Motivated—Part 1

Every animal, from squirrels to lions, is born with a purpose. Whether it's to forage for food, find shelter, or find a mate, they wake up each and every single day knowing exactly what to do to survive. That's their purpose—survival. Our society has removed these challenges for most of us. We're the only animals where work is no longer required for survival and therefore no longer gives us a sense of purpose.

It's our job to replace that with something equally as challenging if we want to feel a sense of being alive.

—MITCH COTE

The past few chapters have been about ways of thinking that can help set you up for success as a first-time founder. But one of the most challenging aspects, and something I get questioned a lot about is: *How do you stay motivated?* Starting a business is a long-term commitment, so how do you stay in that state of mind for such a prolonged period of time? Everybody gets spurts of motivation here or there, but the reality is, a good chunk of the time, motivation is hard to come by.

Like most things, the answer is pretty simple when you really get to the core of the issue. If you want to stay motivated, you need to find a purpose. This chapter is less about a tangible framework and more about giving you an example from my life that helped me realize how much purpose had an impact on my motivation levels, and how learning to channel that helped me keep my mind in a motivated state for longer. But I also realized that if I wanted to be successful as a first-time founder, I needed to be productive even when I wasn't feeling motivated—something that is much easier said than done.

Being honest, I also struggled with this chapter because this was something that I experienced at a young age but didn't fully understand until I was a couple years into truLOCAL. So I'm going to break up the whole connection between motivation and purpose into three chapters: this one, chapter 12 in part III, and chapter 16 in part IV. In this chapter, I'm going to focus on how purpose can fuel your motivation, and then in chapter 12 I'm going to talk about how you can't simply rely on motivation to do good work. This is a personal chapter, and you'll have to find your own way to navigate these learnings. But my hope is that hearing my experience might help you on your journey toward understanding how to leverage motivation through finding your purpose.

Even as I sold my company for almost $17 million, I still thought about all those people throughout my life who put me down and counted me out. We all have them—the teachers, the coaches, the friends, the family, the bosses, the social media stigmas—the people who just don't get you, who think you're weird for not fitting in or for going against the grain, pretty much anybody who criticized us or put us down for doing things differently.

My high school chemistry teacher was one of those people. He may have been a bit of a dick, but I was too back then. I had a huge chip on my shoulder with no filter. In my early years, it wasn't just teachers who I had a problem with. My social life wasn't any better. I was fat and always worried about how I looked. I had a brutal afro, and the fact that I wore women's glasses without even knowing it didn't help. I was completely paranoid to show my face anywhere, knowing that I'd be the perfect target when some cool kid decided to throw out drunk one-liners my way to impress the girls at the party—girls who ironically were always trying just a little too hard to act drunk off three sips of Smirnoff Ice. Needless to say, I didn't really fit in.

Despite that, I always felt like I somehow *knew* myself, even as a teenager in high school. I had a good relationship with my internal dialogue. I knew what I liked and what I wanted. At the time, it might not have been anything worth writing home about. But the things I loved, I *loved*. Gaming was one of them: *Final Fantasy VII, VIII, X; Metal Gear Solid; Gears of War.* The names, characters, story lines, and skill sets I'd developed to master these games were the only things I really cared about.

But out of all those games, there was one game that stood out above the rest. I was the boss at *Halo.* My Xbox gamer tag was even MasterCheif666. This gamer tag is actually a great way to summarize the shambles my life had become after only sixteen years on the planet. I hadn't realized I spelled "Cheif" wrong, and the only reason I had 666 was because at the time six was my favorite number—and MasterCheif6 and MasterCheif66 were already taken, so obviously the next logical step was to try MasterCheif666. But despite my unknowingly botched gamer tag, I did manage to snag the honor of being the number two *Halo 2* player in all of Canada at one point.

I also knew the stuff I didn't like, pretty much anything at all related to school—sitting in class, homework, teachers. I especially didn't like being forced to do things I didn't care about. So when I wouldn't put any effort into anything, my teachers thought I was just too dumb to learn. Realistically, same as with most kids in high school who get labeled as underachievers, I just didn't have any motivation because I wasn't interested in finding the hypotenuse of a triangle, wearing corny uniforms, or any of the generic, cookie-cutter topics taught in schools today.

The only things I really cared about at that point in my life were video games, Yu-gi-oh cards, and anime. And even then, I loved them, but they didn't really fill me with a sense of purpose or anything like that. They just made me happy.

Maybe it was the fact that I was getting a little older. Or maybe I started noticing girls a little more, but out of nowhere—the summer before grade eleven—I decided that I *wanted* things to be different.

> I looked at myself in the mirror and said, "You're done; we're done being a loser. You're better than this."

Every day I woke up miserable, and I was tired of always dealing with bullshit at school. Just because I didn't have a place in the social hierarchical jungle of high school didn't mean I didn't want one. I wanted to have friends. I wanted to be one of the cool kids. And despite how that might sound, I just liked the fact that they were liked and admired. If I'm being honest, I just wanted to be admired too and have people look up to me.

So one day—I'll never forget—I looked at myself in the mirror and said, "You're done; we're done being a loser. You're better than this." I need to pause here to make sure this hits home. I *literally* did this. One day after waking up, knowing that I was probably going to have to deal with some shit that day, I decided I was done with it and went to the mirror and stared at myself as hard as I could, and those were the words that came out. I actually remember saying them out loud. I thought from that moment forward, things were going to be different. And just like that, I believed it. I wish I could turn whatever happened that day in that mirror into some sort of pill, because for whatever reason, from that day on, I carried myself completely differently. This was genuinely the beginning for me, because what came next was what changed my life.

I immediately started thinking about what I could do to transform myself. And I pretty quickly landed on football. I couldn't really tell you why. I knew nothing about football and hadn't even watched a single game. But the one thing I did know is that people respected football players. I had no clue what the rules were, so I bought a few books on football and learned everything I possibly could. The same kid who had zero interest in learning the stuff my teachers wanted me to learn was now crushing books in order to become as knowledgeable about football as possible.

That was where it started, and it started as something superficial, a way for me to feel good about myself. But over the months, I started falling in love with the sport. It no longer became just a way to feel cool; it became a passion. I started getting obsessed. And that moment was when I first started to experience the relationship between purpose and motivation.

I was motivated. I was motivated to do everything and anything to bring me closer to my goals. We all experience the comings and goings of motivation, but this newfound purpose of me playing football kept me consistently motivated for longer than I've ever been in a productive state of motivation before.

That entire summer between grade ten and grade eleven, I went to the gym. I got into shape. I lost weight. I got a haircut. I studied everything I could about football. I also isolated myself from all the negative people, not that I had a lot of friends in my life at the time, anyway. But at least I knew that the fastest way to undermine your road to success is to surround yourself with people who have nothing better to do than talk shit and put you down. I never planned on this, but that actually ended up being one of the best lessons I ever learned.

When I came back to school in the fall, suddenly everyone was wondering where "Dark Marc" went. Dark Marc was a great little nickname that was given to me during my rougher days considering I was the only Black kid at my school at the time. On a sidenote, and as a FU to everyone who used to call me that when I hated the name—I've always carried that name on my email and social handles so that one day when I finally made it, everyone would see that the kid they used to make fun of and call Dark Marc made that name his own and kept stacking up wins despite them trying to use it against me.

Partly from spending all of my time at the gym over the summer, partly from reaping the benefits of a growth spurt, and partly from just getting a decent haircut (it's true what they say, a good haircut can change your life), now everyone wanted to know who the mysterious new guy was—laser-focused on playing football. Seeing as I spent most of my time in the shadows anyway, people literally didn't recognize me.

> Despite the inspirational blog posts and self-help influencers who say otherwise, sacrifice and focus are some of the basic traits you'll need to be a successful first-time founder.

Growing up in the small town of Cornwall, Ontario, there was only rep-league football in the city. The day I went to try out, lo and behold there were all the cool kids—kids from other schools in the city who already had me pegged as a loser for life. As much as my own school was starting to see me differently, these guys had no idea. To them, I was the same old Dark Marc.

I don't know why this moment stuck with me so much, but I'll never forget it. At one point there was a shortage of helmets, and the coach at the time came up to me and asked me to give my helmet to the new quarterback. I said, "Okay, but what about my helmet?"

He looked me dead in the eyes and said, "Beggars can't be choosers." Call me petty, but I promised one day that I'd use that line back on him.

As you can guess, they cut me, which taught me firsthand how everything happens for a reason. I went on to try out for one of the best teams in the league, the Kanata Knights, two hours away, and managed to make that team. Even better, we beat my hometown team, the Cornwall Wildcats, that year. After competing in my first year as a legitimate football player, it solidified how much I loved it. I realized the passion I had for it. And I realized that I wanted to play as much as possible. I loved the feeling that playing football gave me more than anything else. It's something hard to describe to someone who hasn't had this feeling before. It was like every part of me was drawn toward working as hard as possible to make that goal a reality. It was something I could see clearer than day. In fact, it was the clearest I've ever felt about anything. I didn't actually realize it then, but looking back on it now, there was no doubt—playing football had become my *purpose*.

What I realized was, when you have a purpose, no matter the problem you are facing, you find that extra motivation to keep going. You explore every possibility to achieve success. You get creative, think outside the box. You don't mind sacrificing. You don't mind foregoing parties or patio days. And although I'm still reconciling some of these things, you even justify missing birthdays, funerals, and holidays. Because despite the inspirational blog posts and self-help influencers who say otherwise, sacrifice and focus are some of the basic traits you'll need to be a successful first-time founder.

Ultimately, I made it to university and played football. I succeeded because I found something I loved, which at the time became my purpose. The kid who was always lashing out because he had no interests had become passionate about something. I found something I was excited about. I *wanted* to get better. I had a drive to be good. I had a spark that made me want to learn as much as possible. The purpose I had gave me motivation to work harder. The purpose gave me the motivation, which made me willing to put in the work and dedicate all of my time to getting better.

Great articulators can tell you what *their* purpose is in a strong one-liner. Or they can describe what their purpose is in a properly thought-out essay. But to actually describe not what *your* purpose is but *what* purpose is or what purpose does for you, that's something I've struggled with. The best way I can describe it is that purpose is a feeling. It's a desire and a fire so strong that you can't put into words what it does for you. It draws you toward it; you're compelled to chase it. You can't explain it, but if you can't go after it, you obsess over what your life would be like if you could. If you're currently following it, it's all you can think about. There is not one day that goes by that this feeling doesn't cause you to think about your purpose. It's your reason for existing. Because of this indescribable pull and desire, you're motivated to do everything in your power to achieve it. The work no longer feels like a grind because you're motivated to do it.

We all know that feeling when you wake up motivated. You feel like you can take on the world, almost literally. When you're motivated, you wake up and can't jump out of bed fast enough. You start your day with an excitement and energy that's got to feel like Thanos did when he got that final Infinity Stone. You feel like what you're about to accomplish in the day will actually and genuinely move you closer to your goals. And that feeling of potential accomplishment feeds your desire to get to work, which in turn feeds that sense of getting closer to your goals. It's a pretty powerful feedback loop. It makes it so that you immediately want to get to work. You already know that you're going to crush whatever is on your to-do list, whether it be creative like working on a road map, doing content creation on Photoshop, working on tedious stuff like crunching the numbers all day so that you can get your forecast done for investors, or doing performance-based things like closing a big sales call that you've had teed up for a while. You're going to not only get it done, but it's going to feel easy. Contrast this to when you wake up feeling normal or unmotivated, and the thought of even opening your computer feels like a soul-sucking task that needs to be avoided at all costs.

When you're motivated, not only does the quantity of work you're able to get done increase, but maybe most importantly of all, you're happy to be doing it. We've all been there, and we've all experienced it.

Without a purpose, motivation is fleeting. You'll lose interest in your goals and find an excuse not to push forward. Purpose is what will give you a more consistent and constant supply of motivation, which means that the more consistently you're motivated, the more productive you'll be. Realistically, you do your best work when you're motivated; we all know this. You can probably accomplish four times the amount of work when you're motivated rather than when you're not. I've yet to find something that does as good a job at keeping you in a motivated state than truly having a goal that you're so passionate about that it becomes your purpose.

I wish motivation automatically equaled success, but understanding how to leverage motivation to carry you through the long haul of starting a business isn't as simple as just having a strong purpose.

I'm going to end the story here for now and pick back up on my journey with purpose and motivation at the end of the next section. For now, we're going to go back to what you need to be a successful first-time founder. Now that you've got the right mindset, it's time to just get started. The following section is going to address some of the common challenges and roadblocks that you might face after you've started your business.

PART II

All That Matters Is Getting Started

CHAPTER FIVE

Creating Opportunities by Shooting Your Shot and Putting Yourself at the Table

Shooters shoot. The worst thing a shooter can do is think.

—JAMAL CRAWFORD

The mindset and skills that came before this chapter are must-haves. Whether you're good at them or not, there's no avoiding that you'll need them if you want to be a successful first-time founder. This skill, though, is a little different. It's not a deal breaker if you don't take advantage of it. But it's a powerful force multiplier if you do. Even if it **Skill and execution are 49 percent of the equation, and luck is the other 51 percent.** ends up being the difference between your odds of one in a hundred or one in seventy-five, you need to take every advantage you can get.

There's a lot of talk about luck, preparedness, and opportunity. You've probably heard the saying, "Luck is just preparedness plus opportunity." I mentioned in the intro that any real founder can tell you it doesn't matter how smart or skilled you are—luck plays a big role. I'd even venture to say that skill and execution are 49 percent of the equation, and luck is the other 51 percent. Whether you agree with that number or not is up for you to decide. But if we can agree that luck plays a big role, is there a way we can control luck? Or at the very least, can we put ourselves in a position to get lucky more often? We've been doing a good job tackling the "being prepared" portion of luck. This whole book so far has been teaching different ways that you can prepare. If you're reading this, you're probably reading other books as well and have a good understanding that personal development and self-awareness of your strengths and weaknesses are keys to success. Just by doing this, you're increasing your ability to take advantage of the opportunities that come your way. But what about opportunity? How can we increase our exposure to opportunities? Is that something you can also engineer? If you believe that you can, and if you truly feel you're ready to capitalize on any opportunities that come your way, then it's time to start working on ways to increase your exposure to these opportunities.

The two things you can do to increase your exposure to opportunities are

1. shooting your shot and
2. putting yourself at the table.

When it comes to shooting your shot, take this perfect example of when I was in Austin, Texas, recently. I messaged Joe Rogan, letting him know I was going to be in town for a few weeks. I figured he probably gets tons of messages about being on his podcast or people asking for something, so I thought maybe I'll just ask him to hang out. We could go hunting or get a workout in while I was in town. Do I personally know Joe Rogan? No. Does he know me? Definitely not. I know that Joe Rogan gets thousands of messages a day, and the odds of him seeing it, let alone replying, are one in a million. But why not? Just by sending the message, I increased the opportunity from none in a million to one in a million. Small things like this are just examples of how shooting your shot is going to increase your chances of getting lucky. Taking a chance like that, introducing yourself, sending a message—this is how these crazy and unbelievable things happen. Sure, he didn't respond. But what if he did? What if I got a chance to meet with Joe Rogan and we hit it off? I can guarantee that nothing at all would happen if I didn't even try. By shooting my shot, at least there was a chance.

Trying to link up with Joe Rogan might be a long shot, but an example of where this did help me as a first-time founder was with Brittain Ladd.

Brittain Ladd is an absolute powerhouse in the industry. He's a seasoned and highly respected executive and consultant who became the first person to recommend to Amazon it acquire Whole Foods. He played a role in designing Amazon Fresh stores. And he pushed Amazon to think big when it came to groceries. I'd been following his writings for a while on LinkedIn, and I always knew that if I could ever have a conversation with a guy like this, the knowledge and industry insight he could give me would be invaluable. I figured, what did I have to lose by shooting my shot? Back on Christmas Eve of 2018, I sent him a message on LinkedIn, letting him know I was a huge fan of his writing, that it was helping me a lot as an operator, and that his insights were genuinely giving me a heads-up on industry changes and headwinds. I thanked him for the great articles he posts and wished him a Merry Christmas. Guess what happened? He actually responded:

"Thanks for the kind words, and for reading the articles. Feel free to use any of the content you need. Merry Christmas."

My first thought was: *Sweet, he responded. But how can I step this up a notch?* So I waited a week or so and sent him another message on LinkedIn. It just so happened to be on New Year's Day. Here is the exact message I wrote:

> *"Hey Brittain, Happy New Year! I'm sure you'll be working towards some ambitious goals throughout 2019. I have a wishful ask. Like I said above, I just randomly stumbled across your article on LinkedIn and since following you I'm literally blown away by your content. The New Year's Day ask is wondering if there's any chance I could take 15 minutes of your time, just to get your 2 cents on our current space and if there's any room for acquisition. We're still a relatively small start up and I'm not sure full consultation is within our budget. But if there's anything I could do to repay the 15 minutes of your time, please let me know. I may not be able to offer anything of value right now, but hopefully in the future as I grow as a founder and gain more experience, there's a way I'll be able to repay the favor. Figured I'd toss this out there and take a chance to kick off 2019!"*

Five minutes later, while I was standing in our warehouse packing boxes on January 1, 2019, my phone pinged. I looked down to see a message from Brittain. It simply said, "Call me," and included his phone number.

Since then, I've had multiple conversations with Brittain, and I consider him a mentor. As a first-time founder, words can't express the value of having access to guidance from someone like him. Shooting your shot might sound obvious, but until you hear about the results that can come from something as simple as sending a message, you don't realize the impact.

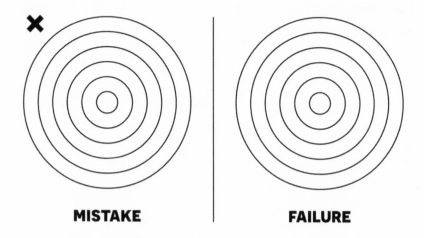

MISTAKE | **FAILURE**

Shooting your shot alone can definitely help, but another skill I've developed is the ability to put myself at the table. A couple examples of times this has paid off are with Michele Romanow, CEO of the Canadian unicorn Clearco and the e-commerce guru from *Dragons' Den*, and Naveen Jain, the billionaire founder of Viome.

I need to preface this by saying, as a founder, we tend to live and breathe the saying, "jack of all trades, master of none." We're problem solvers. We use the resources at our disposal to get things done, which works well as a leader. We do also tend to have some personality traits that can serve us pretty well as well. I'd recommend you find yours and lean into them. For me, I've always been known to be overly persistent. I like the word persistent because it sounds a lot better than saying I do a good job of being tastefully annoying. When I want something, I can get pretty annoying about it. But for me, understanding the power of turning that into a positive trait helped me lean into it. Most people would look at being annoying as a flaw and try to suppress it. I've always been a believer that you're the best version of yourself when you lean into more of what you are, the good things and the bad things, rather than trying to balance yourself based on society's opinions. So instead of leaning away from it, I leaned into it and discovered that I could use this to my advantage. I think leaning into persistence is what really helped me get value out of "putting myself at the table."

The first example was with Michele Romanow. If you're not aware, *Dragons' Den* is Canada's version of *Shark Tank*. The premise of the show is pretty much the same: up-and-coming entrepreneurs try to pitch the next big idea to a panel of multimillionaire business moguls, hoping one or all might invest. When you land a deal on these shows, the real negotiations happen after the pitch. For Michele and me, that was an eight-month process. We were literally going back and forth for months, and I didn't even get to meet Michele until probably five months into it because she had her business partner—who was an expert negotiator—get the deal laid out. Not to my surprise, but nine times out of ten, after we'd meet, the conversation would die. Me as the "asking" party looking for something, it was my job to keep the conversation going.

It would happen like this: we'd have dinner and be pushing back and forth on finer points of the deal. Or they would take us out on their sailboat and do a deep dive, trying to understand if our business was the real deal or not. It was always a battle, us explaining why we deserve a deal and them using their experience to try and poke holes in our execution or business model. Then we'd part ways because they needed to review some things internally and get back to us.

After a few encounters like this, it became obvious to me that if I wanted this deal to happen, I was going to have to consistently and persistently force myself to the table to keep the conversation going. What do you think would have happened if I had just let it go and left it up to them to reach back out? If I just rolled over and told people, "Well, they never called me back, so we're just waiting on that." Or worse, if I used that as the excuse for not closing the deal. Well, for starters, I likely wouldn't be writing this book right now.

Eventually, it got to the point where I would just start inviting myself over to their place and make them have to deal with me. I actually remember one time hanging out in their lobby to ambush them. Luckily for me, they were good sports about it. At the end of the day, I needed them; they didn't need me. They probably have a million deals coming their way. This was a huge opportunity to supercharge truLOCAL, and if I wasn't doing everything in my power to sprint toward this opportunity, I wasn't doing my job as a founder. Ultimately, we got the deal done. And as a testament to Michele's experience as an operator, I believe she has her team and her process set up that way on purpose—to weed out people who aren't driven and persistent. Needless to say, Michele and her team were a huge value-add to my growth as a first-time founder after the success we all had with the acquisition of truLOCAL. Today, I feel like I owe a lot of my success to her. She never left us hanging, always messaged back, and always had our back. That experience was one of my deeper learnings and really helped me validate that turning my annoyingness into a strength was warranted.

Another time when "put yourself at the table" paid off for me was the first time I met a billionaire in real life. Naveen Jain, among other things (including having the first commercial space mission to the moon in 2017), is the founder of Viome, and I met him almost by accident. I had been invited to a three-day networking event called the Archangel Mastermind, hosted by my now friend Giovanni Marsico—basically a community of heavy hitters who get together at a private conference with their focus and mission to be change makers in the world, to learn from one another, and get recentered on what life after success is all about.

Still being pretty early in truLOCAL, I was invited as a (much appreciated) pity offer by a mutual friend who thought I was working on some cool things. And because I was relatively young, he figured why not toss me an invite. At the conference, they had all sorts of rock star influencers and entrepreneurs attend and present the keynote speeches. I was definitely out of my weight class, so I didn't know anybody there at all. I was pretty much always sitting by myself, just being a fly on the wall and listening, which I didn't mind. By the last day, I had done a decent job of making some connections, but I remember Naveen Jain being the last speaker and keynote. I also remember connecting the dots that if all these people who are already millionaires and business moguls are here to listen and learn from this guy, he must be the real deal. While he was up there on stage speaking, I thought, "Man, this is it—this is the guy I need to talk to. If nothing else, I just need to let him know who I am."

So I started problem-solving. If I wanted to have a real chat with this guy, I needed to get him alone. How do you get a billionaire alone? I had no idea, but I figured I'd just problem solve it along the way. As soon as I saw his keynote was winding down, I went out into the hall to wait for him to come out. Of course, to my disappointment, thirty other people and I had the same idea. The thing about billionaires is that everywhere they go, their team and other people just coalesce around them. They're like aircraft carriers in the center of a strike group. When they turn left, battleships, destroyers, and subs all turn with them.

He eventually came out with his army of people, stood in the hall, and a circle of no less than twenty people formed around him. I stood in the circle, waiting for everyone to ask their questions. And I waited. And I waited. People started to leave, but I kept lingering and watching. Then it whittled down to about twelve people or so, and he said something to his people like, "All right, it's lunchtime. Let's go grab something to eat." This happened to be a group lunch event with all these different tables, so I just kind of followed the little entourage of twelve people. No one knew who I was, but no one was asking questions, so I just kept my mouth shut and acted like I belonged.

It was a buffet-style lunch. Everyone got their food, and I just kept following along. There was no assigned seating, so everyone just grabbed their own table, which were these big, circular-style tables that fit about ten people. I spotted what table Naveen was headed toward, so I made sure to quickly stand by a chair at the table to secure a spot before it filled up. Naveen got to his table, and all of his people sat down, so I sat too. At this point I was feeling pretty good—at the very least now I was sitting at the same table with this billionaire, and nobody seemed to wonder who I was. Everyone started eating, so I ate and watched him. At that point I figured the next steps would be to wait until everyone left and maybe I'd have my chance with him.

Eventually, lunch wound down, and one by one, people started to leave. Then it was just me and him and one other person sitting at the table. Almost out of no where, for the first time his focus turned to me and he broke a grin and said, "So, what do you want to ask me?" As though fulfilling every pedestal and belief I had about what type of person you need to be to become a billionaire, things don't slip by these guys. He knew I was some random there the whole time.

We started chatting, and he was more than willing to have a conversation. I ended up keeping the conversation going, because I knew the longer we spoke, the more I was increasing my odds of building a relationship and creating opportunities. I told him about my business. He explained a little about his new venture. I told him

I also did consulting on digital strategy on the side. He didn't ask anything about that at the time, but he did ask if I wanted to switch the scenery and grab a coffee.

Now it was just me and him, going to get coffee and shooting the shit. From a preparedness standpoint, I always have a list of questions that I'd ask any celebrities or businesspeople who I get the opportunity to meet. I always see people who get these opportunities to meet their heroes or mentors and then just fumble the ball, telling them how big of a fan they are or asking for a photo. If you get these opportunities, be prepared. Make sure you have something to talk about that makes them see you're not like everyone else.

As a tip for this, focus on getting their opinion rather than asking questions. For me, it's always about getting their perspective on what I'm doing or getting an idea of what they would do or what they see as opportunities if they were in my shoes. Although Naveen had infinite resources, something in our conversation must have given him a little bit of confidence in me, because when I shot my shot and asked if he'd let me take a once-over of his marketing campaign and provide some opinions, he said *yes*. Some would say an opportunity like that was lucky. But I'll always know that it was me putting myself at the table that created the *opportunity* for me to get lucky.

> Make sure you have something to talk about that makes them see you're not like everyone else.

I can't teach you to sit down with a billionaire. I can't teach you to follow up nonstop with someone. But hopefully these anecdotes demonstrate the power of shooting your shot and putting yourself at the table, and the things that can happen when you do. These examples are some of the bigger ones, but this kind of thing happens to me on a weekly basis.

When you're a first-time founder, creating every opportunity you can to find a mentor, to talk with someone who might want to invest in your business, or to just connect with industry insiders is critical. Increasing exposure to opportunities is more of a mindset. It's saying to yourself: *Why the hell not?* What's the worst that can happen? Someone tells you *no*? So you are no better and no worse than you were before. All it takes is one *yes* to pay out a lifetime of dividends.

Putting yourself at the table and shooting your shot means creating an opportunity that otherwise wouldn't exist. It doesn't just mean reaching out to influencers like Joe Rogan either. It could be seizing an opportunity to jump into a meeting with higher-level people, like managers for example. Maybe you started a new job, and when the owner or the CEO is walking by, you make a point to say something like, "Hey, listen, I just started today and have a long way to go, but I'm going to be your highest performer. Just want to let you know to keep an eye out." It could be firing off a cold LinkedIn message to someone who you would like to have for a mentor.

There's no real skill in putting yourself at the table, and it's completely free. It's also different from taking a risk. It just takes the courage to do it and the lack of ego to accept rejection gracefully. Even if there's a 0.000001 percent chance that it's going to happen, if it doesn't compromise your ethics or put you in danger, then why not? You don't have to wait around for luck to hit you. Like everything else in business, you can influence the direction.

CHAPTER SIX

Avoid Cofounder Drama with Difficult Conversations and a Shareholders' Agreement

Rule III: Do not hide unwanted things in the fog.

—JORDAN PETERSON

First-time founders always think the biggest threat to their business is going to come from the outside. They worry that one of their competitors is going to come up with a breakthrough that lets them dominate the market. Or someone else is going to raise a bunch of money and start competing more aggressively. Or maybe the boogeyman keeping them up at night is a supply chain disruption. The reality is that the biggest threat to any new business is way closer to home: cofounder drama.

It sounds petty, but cofounder drama is a cancer that can cause all the success and momentum of a new business to stall out. This can be as simple as day-to-day bickering or constant disagreements that can derail progress over time. Not to mention, that kind of behavior undermines a company's culture, which puts a strain on attracting and retaining good talent.

A lot of things can cause cofounder drama, but where I've seen the most dangerous cofounder drama come up is from a lack of respect, where egos start coming into play. When that happens, either decisions get held up or end up being driven by one-upping the other founder instead of what is best for the business. This ends up being a slippery slope, and you'd be surprised at how fast this can devolve into the worst-case scenario of getting into a legal battle with your cofounder. Someone wants their shares back. Someone wants to leave. Someone wants to start a competing company. They might try to steal talent. Or worse, they embezzle money or commit fraud. Cofounder drama can get very ugly, very quickly.

You already have so many things working against you as a first-time founder. Even if you *do* make all the right decisions, you still have a huge chance of failure. Imagine trying to run a successful business while not only fending off all the external threats but also fighting your cofounder every step of the way. It's a complete and total waste of energy, motivation, and momentum.

Listen, I know what you're probably thinking: *My cofounder* (or cofounders if you have more than one) *is different. This is my friend. This is my family. You don't understand; we trust each other. That will never happen to us.* Sorry, but you and your cofounder, no matter how close, are no exception to the rule. You may be friends and on the same page right now, but one thing I can guarantee you've never experienced together is making decisions *after* a significant amount of risk, labor, opportunity, or success enters the picture.

Investing your time, energy, and ideas is one thing. It's easy to be agreeable when nothing but hope is on the table. But you'd be surprised how quickly and radically things suddenly change when the ball starts rolling and money gets involved. The worst possible mistake any first-time founder can make is thinking that they can deal with all the details later. Because when later comes, and you and your cofounder are dealing with big-ticket customers or investors looking to cut checks, it's too late to deal with it. It doesn't matter who you are—all humans tend to start thinking more deeply and more selfishly about things when money gets involved. To pause and be clear, I'm not saying that your cofounder is out to get you; it's just human nature. Your ability to negotiate with one another is going to be vastly different when you are starting off with an idea that you're mutually excited about versus when there's $100,000 on the table. All of a sudden, someone might start thinking they deserve more because they did more of X, Y, or Z.

You and your future cofounder can discuss and dream and plan all day and night. But when it comes down to putting money in and/ or quitting your day jobs and/or incorporating the business, before you take anything a single step further, you need to have what I call the "bullshit conversations."

It's not particularly eloquent, but I call them the bullshit conversations because they are the conversations nobody wants to have. They suck. They're annoying. They can be tense and awkward, and most of the time, first-time founders tend to avoid them and sweep them under the rug—hence "bullshit conversations." But they are absolutely necessary, and if you get them out of the way right off the bat, you and your cofounder can add an extra layer of alignment, accountability, and protection.

Imagine a situation where you're a year into the business. Things are going well. You both have invested the time, money, and risk into the business, and you're actually achieving a certain level of success. You're ahead of your competitors, and customers are flowing in. That's not to say that it was easy to get to this point. It probably took a lot of effort and focus. Your tenacity and work ethic, strategy and execution, and a little bit of luck have kept you ahead of your competition. But as you know, a lead is only a lead for however long you can maintain the momentum.

Despite things going well, you begin to notice that one of your cofounders starts showing up late to meetings. You don't think it's an issue at first, but then you start to notice that the things assigned to that individual are falling through the cracks. Your cofounder seems a little more distant, less willing to take on their share of work. Eventually, they start missing meetings altogether. You alone, or with the rest of your cofounders, do what you need to do and pick up the slack, but you see that it's becoming a problem. You get that "spidey sense" that founders get when they know something bad is brewing.

Like clockwork, your cofounder asks for a meeting where they let you know they've decided to take an opportunity elsewhere. You wish you could be in shock, but what you're really feeling is a frustrated sense of denial. "Well, you can't. We're already in this deep; you can't just up and leave. What about all the things that need to be done? What about your projects and promises that you made to vendors and customers that you're responsible for?" These are all the things that you'll be thinking before the anger sets in. "Well, fine. Whatever. Go. Just give us back the passwords to the accounts. We'll take your name off the bank account, and obviously we'll need those shares back." Then, the response that you've been dreading. You can't believe you hear it, but at the same time you can.

"What are you talking about?" they say. "Those shares are mine. I've put in the same work you have this past year." And so it begins.

Think about a scenario where you and your cofounder start a business and it is going great. You formally create the company, and each founder receives an equal share of the equity. You're in this together after all—equal founders and shareholders and equal participants. It makes total sense. Now, your cofounder is leaving the company after a year, just when you're really starting to build the team and get traction. Should that founder walk away with 50 percent of the business after only twelve months of work? Say you stick it out and run the business day and night for five more years—should they receive the same proceeds once you sell the business? If you don't have a proper vesting arrangement in place when you organize the company (vesting being where the shares are unlocked over a period of time, usually four years, rather than being assigned right away), this could be the unfortunate situation you find yourself in.

These issues may not creep up right away, but if you never have the bullshit conversations, it is just a matter of time before they do. And more likely than not, if you're not experienced with how to navigate these types of situations, it can devolve into a worst-case scenario of personal attacks. At that point, the chances of a peaceful reconciliation are pretty far off. As cofounders, you're the leaders of the organization, and if you think issues among cofounders won't be picked up by the rest of the team, you're being naive. If the situation gets bad enough, and loud enough, the rest of the team, whether consciously or unconsciously, are going to be affected or, worse, feel the need to choose sides. Then the business becomes fragmented. To take it one step further, you don't have a shareholders' agreement or vesting arrangements in place (which I'll explain soon), because you didn't want to have the bullshit conversation, and you figured you would just sort things along the way in real time. So that means you can't

> **As cofounders, you're the leaders of the organization, and if you think issues among cofounders won't be picked up by the rest of the team, you're being naive.**

even legally go after this person for the shares. It's likely you don't know if *they* know that fact. You don't even know what you don't know, so now you have to go down a rabbit hole to try to figure all of it out. And never forget, this is on top of the day-to-day stress of pushing your business forward.

Scary scenario, but the good news is you can avoid this situation with just two things: a bullshit conversation and a shareholders' agreement. Taking the latter first, what exactly is a shareholders' agreement? Just because you incorporate a company doesn't mean you automatically have a shareholders' agreement. Incorporating the company just means you've created a legal entity. And yes, you'll choose who gets how many shares when you incorporate the company, but there needs to be a set of rules assigned to those shares. Otherwise, it's a matter of he said, she said.

A shareholders' agreement outlines the rules for the shares. When and how long do you have them? Do their shares vest? Are they all assigned right away? What happens in the case of a disagreement? What powers do the shares have? Although these details seem complicated, they're really not. As a first-time founder, 95 percent of the time you are going to use the most standard clauses that are in a typical shareholders' agreement. And they are also infinitely customizable if you need to get more complex.

With all of that being said, I'm not a lawyer, and this perspective is coming from my own experiences. But the value of understanding these concepts is so important that I wanted to make sure to get you as much accurate information as possible. So to properly describe various aspects of a shareholders' agreement, I asked Kyle Lavender, partner at LaBarge Weinstein, one of the top corporate law firms in the country, to give us some notes that will help you as a first-time founder looking to dive into your first shareholders' agreement.

Founders' Agreements: The Minimum Viable Legals for Founders

Kyle Lavender – Partner, LaBarge Weinstein

Regardless of your size, stage, or experience, there are three critical items that need to be addressed by the founders when organizing your company:

1. **Founder vesting**. Will founders own their shares without any restrictions (which isn't recommended), or will the company have the right to repurchase shares from a departing founder?
2. **Board of directors**. How many people are going to be on the board, and who decides the board composition?
3. **Sale of the company**. When selling your business, who decides when it should be sold, and at what point can you force other shareholders (cofounders or otherwise) to sell their shares?

FOUNDER VESTING

The gold standard for a start-up organization is to have a vesting arrangement in place with your cofounders. Vesting generally means that you will receive your shares on day one, but the company has the right to repurchase all or a portion of these shares in the future on a "triggering event." The right to repurchase these shares, or the "triggering event," generally occurs when a founder is no longer active in the business. This may happen when a founder resigns, or if the relationship doesn't work and the founder is terminated. Although this is less likely, it does happen, and you should prepare for this scenario.

The common approach to vesting is a four-year vesting period, with a one-year cliff. This means that if a founder leaves within one year of the vesting start date, the company can repurchase all of the shares the founder owns in the business. This generally occurs at the price the founder pays for the shares, which is usually one dollar, or a similar nominal amount. There is also the possibility for this vesting arrangement to be accelerated on a change of control. This generally works for founders since they've made their commitment to the firm and achieved the intended goal for the business. It is less common for later-stage employees, who may have only been with the company for a year and might not have earned the full equity grant that was given to them.

Vesting isn't just important for founders but for employees as well. The vesting concept should apply to all equity grants, with the exemption of investors. When issuing shares or stock options to early-stage employees, everyone should be subject to the same vesting schedule. This ensures that everyone is in a unified and aligned commitment to the company going forward, and you can't game the system. You need to work to earn your equity in the business, without exception.

Vesting arrangements are crucial for two reasons: (1) it is an important tool for retention during the difficult start-up phase, and (2) it protects the other founders by knowing they will still be incentivized to work hard and grow the business even if a key founder and shareholder leaves the company.

BOARD OF DIRECTORS

As mentioned above, the board of directors controls the most important aspects of any company. When it comes to hiring or firing the CEO, completing a debt, equity financing, or acquiring another business, the board as a whole makes these decisions. It is important to note that the board also decides when to repurchase unvested shares from a founder. As a result, the parties that control the board are the same people who can independently decide to terminate you and repurchase any unvested shares. This is an important consideration when you have vesting arrangements in place and bring on outside investors and board members.

Shareholders' agreements commonly fix the size of the board of directors. It may be one person for an early-stage start-up or three founders on the organization of the company. Either way, there are generally two ways in which the board members are appointed. The first is simply that an individual founder can nominate and appoint a member of the board. This is usually the founder personally. The second is that shareholders who hold a certain proportion of shares (or a particular series or class of shares) can appoint directors. This is a little more common when you have third-party investors such as a venture capital fund that would hold a different class of shares (usually preferred shares, as opposed to common shares).

If you have a cofounder when starting your business, and you share equity equally, it might make sense to have each of you on the board. However, it is important to remember that any approval at the board level will require the consent of a majority of the members of the board. As a result, companies that have two-person boards don't have an easy conflict resolution mechanism. If there is a disagreement, and the board is split on the matters, a costly and lengthy court proceeding may be required to decide the next steps for the business. As such, it is common to have an odd number of directors.

Regardless of how your shareholders' agreement is structured, board appointments for founders should be conditional on the founder's continued engagement with the business as an active employee. If someone resigns from the company or moves to a beautiful island in the Caribbean, it is less than ideal to require that individual's input and consent to complete a transaction that may be critical to the business. It can cause excessive delays administratively and can be demoralizing for the team as a whole.

Remember that your share allocation early on is tied to how much of the company you own and how much you will profit from the sale of the business. Your board seat and the board composition dictate how much control of the company you have. As a result, it is crucial to closely negotiate in a shareholders' agreement how the board will be nominated and how to manage the board of directors on an ongoing basis.

SALE OF THE COMPANY

For most start-ups, a successful outcome is to get acquired. After years of hard work, it is the validation of the business and the liquidity that shareholders are waiting for. Although this will likely occur years after you initially incorporate your business, it is important to plan for this goal from day one.

When negotiating an acquisition, founders are commonly surprised to find that all shareholders are required to sign a share purchase agreement. This is the agreement by which the shares are sold to the acquiring company. Since each shareholder is required to sell their shares, all shareholders must sign the agreement. If shareholders holding 95 percent of the shares agree to sign the share purchase agreement, and 5 percent of shareholders hold out, it could be a deal killer. It isn't that you can't sell your business without unanimous shareholder approval. It is just much more complicated and usually worse from a tax perspective.

Each shareholder's agreement should contain a "drag" provision, or a "drag-along right." Essentially, the agreement will outline the required threshold to approve a sale of the company. Once the applicable threshold is approved, the other shareholders are legally obligated to sign the agreement (subject to certain caveats). There is commonly a power of attorney introduced as well, so that the company could sign certain materials on behalf of these holdout shareholders.

There's a lot to consider when you're putting together your shareholders' agreement, and like most people, first-time founders sometimes tend to drift toward the path of least resistance. So where do you even start with a shareholders' agreement? Well, this is where the bullshit conversations come in.

Before even discussing the shareholders' agreement, you need to start the bullshit conversation, which is made up of three topics that you need to sit down and openly discuss with your cofounder. The number one thing to understand here is that these conversations need to be fully flushed out. It's not over until full alignment is reached between all the parties involved. If you have to revisit the topic multiple times, that's fine. But you can't move forward until each topic is resolved. More often than not, if you all lay your cards on the table and have a truly transparent conversation, you can align around a plan that works for everyone.

First Topic: Decide What Kind of Business You Want

Have a serious, point-blank conversation about alignment in terms of what you want out of the business. Do you want a lifestyle business where you grow organically, or a venture-backed business where you dilute and raise a ton of cash? Do you want a long-term cash cow, or do you want to move to acquisition within two years? You all need to understand one another's goals before you even begin, because otherwise you'll be two years in, and someone might be looking to cash out while you were just getting started. So sit down and make sure that you're on the same page in terms of what you want the business to be. If you're all on the same page, great. If not, that's what these conversations are for.

> If you all lay your cards on the table and have a truly transparent conversation, you can align around a plan that works for everyone.

Second Topic: Decide and Define Your Roles

It's very, very, *very* important that cofounders have clearly defined roles. Of course, you're all going to wear multiple hats, and you're going to help each other get things done. But you need to make absolutely sure that there is a certain set of responsibilities that land on individual A and individual B (and C and D, if that's the case). The great thing about this topic is it will also touch on complementary skill sets. Complementary skill sets are an important factor when figuring out who your cofounders are going to be, and sometimes it's hard to tell what each person brings to the table. This conversation can help flush out that for you.

Third Topic: Decide Compensation and Equity Split

Now is the time for numbers. Are you going 50/50? Is it 70/30? You're not getting paid anyway as a first-time founder, so equity splits are important. To prevent a headache later, make sure to decide what the split is going to be. Let's assume there are just two of you, and you want to go 50/50. Believe it or not, it can be a huge mistake and a major red flag if you don't have a proper shareholders' agreement and vesting arrangement in place. Maybe from a financial perspective you can have equal compensation. But for efficiency and to avoid roadblocks, you're better off agreeing to a 49/51 percent split. Because if you go 50/50 and you both can't come to an agreement on something, you are gridlocked. Now you stalled out because you can't make a decision. But if you or your cofounder can agree to give one of you that extra percentage point of power, disaster is always averted because decisions can be made. This isn't necessarily an easy conversation. So make sure that you come with well-thought-out points. And make sure to facilitate an open-minded conversation by letting every person involved voice their opinion. Also, if you remember from Kyle's points, control boils down to the board.

If one of you holds 51 percent of the shares, and you don't have a shareholders' agreement or similar agreement in place, that individual will be able to control who is on the board.

You can have one director or many directors. Contrary to what many founders believe, your share allocation doesn't give you the power in the company you're looking for. The most important decisions in a company happen at the board level, and each board member has one vote regardless of the number of shares that person may hold in the company (if any). For instance, if you have 60 percent of the shares in a company and your cofounder holds 40 percent, but each of you has the right to appoint one director under the shareholders' agreement, both of you will have the same power at the board level. So it's important to clearly spell out your equity splits and board control to avoid or account for power struggles that could potentially come up in the future.

Just by covering these three topics, you can not only show your cofounder that you're diligent and respectful of what matters to them, but you'll also show them that mutual understanding and respect are important to you. Once the bullshit conversations are complete, you're ready to build out your shareholders' agreement, which can be described in the simplest way as a legal form that will help formalize some of the things you discussed in your bullshit conversations, specifically around compensation and how the shares will work.

When all of these steps are followed—and with a shareholders' agreement in place—you and your cofounder are automatically in a better position than a team who decided to push these off. These guidelines will disincentivize unethical behavior, hold everyone accountable, and prevent most misunderstandings and confrontations from happening in the first place.

Bottom line, you've got to treat your business like a transaction. You and your cofounders can be friends, you can be family, but you need to treat it like a business because it *is* a business.

I get asked a lot what to look for in a cofounder, and a lot of people immediately go to "someone who I get along with." Being someone who thrives and strives for argument, I always found that interesting. I think that the best ideas can only come from arguments. One of my biggest fears is being surrounded by people who are "yes" people. People who agree with everything you say—that's always a major red flag to me. You want to be challenged; you want your ideas proven wrong; you want to have different perspectives completely break down the way you think. And for that reason, while "getting along" with your cofounder is a "nice to have," it was never something I thought was a "must-have."

The thing that you *need* to have for your cofounder, however, is mutual respect. It's a bonus if you get along well, but liking each other is not a prerequisite. The prerequisite is mutual respect. As long as you have mutual respect with that individual, you can go to battle together. You can go at each other head-to-head and make sure that the best ideas get implemented. When you've got mutual respect between yourself and your cofounder, you will always come out doing what's best for the business, which is ultimately what's best for you and the rest of the team.

CHAPTER SEVEN

The Truth about Early-Stage Hires

A fool is one who thinks his empire was built alone.

—PATRICE NGUYEN

So now you and your cofounder are making it happen, the start-up is gaining some momentum, and you realize that if you want to hit that next level, you're going to need some help. Essentially, you're at a point where hiring your first employees makes sense. This is a really tough moment for first-time founders because usually it means bringing on a whole new type of expense that you're not used to. Deciding to start taking on employee salaries isn't an easy decision, but more often than not, it's one that you have to make if you want to start leveraging your time and growing your business. I've talked to a lot of first-time founders about this, and the biggest question I hear at this stage is whether to

1. spend more and hire for experience, *or*
2. spend less, sacrifice some of the experience, and hire for enthusiasm or hustle instead.

EXPERIENCE	ENTHUSIASM
IMMEDIATE CONTRIBUTION	JACK OF ALL TRADES
INDUSTRY CONNECTIONS	EXCITED TO LEARN
SYSTEMS AND PROCESSES	WILLING TO GO THE EXTRA MILE

There are obviously lots of pros and cons with either option. With an experienced hire, you get exactly what you are paying for—*experience*. That individual can provide long-range vision and cost-saving strategies. They can optimize and organize your operations and often have a lot of good ideas that can help your business operate smoother, at least on paper. The thing is more often than not these types of individuals will often expect a team to work with in order to get the job done. At this stage in their career, they aren't going to necessarily want to roll up their sleeves and get into the nitty-gritty of executing their plan. And at this stage of your business, you need people to roll up their sleeves.

> The thing I find most impressive in the people I interview is how excited they are about the company.

As a start-up, you are typically running super lean. Anyone you hire is likely going to need to be okay doing exactly what you've been doing—working late nights, wearing multiple hats, figuring out solutions on the fly, and just overall being willing to sit with you in the trenches. This isn't to say that you can't find someone with high-level experience who can actively contribute to the strategic vision *and* be willing to do the heavy lifting. They just tend to be few and far between and also have a price tag that is representative of their skills.

Option 2, saving money and hiring for enthusiasm or hustle, also has pros and cons. When it comes to saving money and trying to find someone who's willing to work as your first or second employee, you need to start by giving up the expectation of experience. If you aren't able or aren't willing to pay people for their experience, then you need to start looking at other skills that can make up for their lack of experience. This is where enthusiasm and hustle come in.

I've sat in many interviews, and I can confidently say that the thing I find most impressive in the people I interview is how excited they are about the company or position. Do they care about the business, and did they do the research? Do they know the brand or the culture? Do they start to glow a little when they talk about the company? Are they taking notes? I'll never forget an interview where the person we were interviewing said the thing they were most excited about with truLOCAL was the length in which our employees stayed employed with us based on their LinkedIn pages. We immediately felt like this person was in the interview for the right reasons. These are all things I'm keying in on while sitting with someone who might be more inexperienced than other candidates.

So if the con of option 2 is the lack of experience and the pro is enthusiasm and hustle, it's important to know that it's then *your* job to step up to the responsibility of training this individual. I've seen many founders make the mistake of hiring an individual for enthusiasm but then expect them to immediately perform at the level in which an experienced person would. Don't set yourself and your new candidate up for failure by having an unrealistic expectation of them. You decided on the trade-off; now you need to lean in and accept the pros of having an enthusiastic individual who's willing to put down the hours and is eagerly willing to learn and drop the expectation of having someone come in and immediately make a strategic impact.

I can confidently say that there have been many times where I've gone with the more enthusiastic individual over the more experienced individual, especially in the first couple years when money was tight.

So if you've decided that enthusiasm is the most affordable and most realistic solution, how does a first-time founder go about finding people who will be genuinely enthusiastic about their business? This is where I get to dispel one of the popular myths surrounding first-time founders: don't buy into the myth of *never hire friends*. Seriously, you being a daydreaming entrepreneur turned first-time founder, your friends more likely than not have already been putting up with your ranting and daydreaming for years—for *free*. These are the people who have been supporting you from day one and have already been in your corner advocating for your business. If you get to the size where you're able to hire an individual and you have a friend who you trust, on paper it's an opportunity for a win-win. But typically, founder cliché makes it so that most first-time founders don't even explore the option.

> Your friends more likely than not have already been putting up with your ranting and daydreaming for years—for *free*. These are the people who have been supporting you from day one and have already been in your corner advocating for your business.

Look, I know the horror stories out there about hiring friends. When things go sideways, it gets messy, and the whole friendship can end up in shambles. Or because they're friends, they take advantage of the situation. Maybe you're worried that they won't respect you as a leader or as a boss because you were friends first. These are all valid concerns. But I truly believe if you weigh out the pros and cons, the upside potential of being able to work with friends makes it worth exploring.

When it came to truLOCAL, we built the business up to sixty team members. I can confidently say one of the proudest facts of all is that at the time of this writing, all our first ten employees were friends and friends of friends, and all were still with the business five years later at the time of acquisition. We may not be perfect, but we've done an amazing job of team building and creating a culture that made people feel appreciated, empowered, and supported.

So with that being said, here's a summary of the reasons why I think, as a first-time founder, you should at least entertain the idea of working with some of the friends in your life who have the skill set or the enthusiasm to help you grow your business.

As a First-Time Founder, You Need Horsepower

Honestly, starting off, you don't need a ton of experience. Yes, the old saying, "work smarter, not harder," is always good advice. But in those early months, you just need the hard work part. You need that extra horsepower, and you just need to execute. That means you need people who are willing to work and not sit around contemplating how to make things run better and more efficient. There's a time and a place for that, and eventually you will be at a point where you want to work smarter, not harder. But in the early days, hiring friends who care about you and your business will give you that extra horsepower that will be difficult to find elsewhere.

As a First-Time Founder, You Need Buy-In

The next thing you're going to need is someone who actually gives a shit about you and your vision. Because once again, the whole concept of hiring friends who care means that there's someone around who—when something goes wrong at 10:00 p.m.—you can call to go into problem-solving mode with you. They need to be understanding and sympathetic. They really have to care. Think about who is truly going to care the most about your baby besides you. Your real friends and family.

As a First-Time Founder, You Need the Family/Friend Discount

Last but not least—and to address the elephant in the room—you need someone who is willing to work for lower pay than they would normally accept. Friends and family are the ones who *may* be willing to give you the greatest gift and advantage of all, by being more likely to work for you at a discount than they will for someone else. During those first couple of years at truLOCAL, I literally used to sit in every single interview with my friends and point-blank ask them: "How do you feel about being overworked and underpaid?" It's harsh, and it won't win any motivation speech awards, but I always wanted to be honest about what they were getting into.

That's not to say that, by taking a pay cut to work for you, you can't offer anything in return. There needs to be the possibility of an upside, even if it is way down the road. You need to lay out the value they're going to get if they take you up on the offer. You can offer them the valuable experience of being part of growing a business from the ground up. Maybe they are interested in starting their own business someday, and now they have the opportunity to watch all the trials and errors happen in real time without the risk.

Additionally, if they decide to get in on the ground floor, you can assure them of the opportunity to grow within the business that they helped to build. As the business grows, they can take on higher positions in the company. And then, as the business really takes off, you can sweeten the pot with raises, higher-level positions, bonuses, benefits, and shares. Whatever you do and whatever you decide, the most critical thing is to make sure to keep your promises. And to always be transparent. If things are going bad, tell them it's bad. If things are going better than expected, share that with them too.

If you're seriously going to build something big, why wouldn't you want your friends and family involved? These are the people who you trust, the people who you feel will go the extra mile to help you succeed. Why wouldn't you want to win together? Why wouldn't you want the friends who believed in you and stood by your side to share in the glory?

We hired friends because we had an ideology of working together for the team, not working for the business. Because at the end of the day, a company's culture is built from the top. The reason we had success is because people didn't just show up every day to work for the business or to service our customers. We built a culture around working hard for one another. That's something you can only do when you work with friends.

CHAPTER EIGHT

Working with Freelancers, Dev Houses, and Marketing Agencies

Nobody is going to care as much about your business as you will.

—ALEN BRCANOVIC

At some point soon after you've gotten your business off the ground, there's no doubt that you and your cofounder are going to need expertise in areas that fall well beyond the skill sets of you and your team. This is where you are going to need to make another tough decision and face another rite of passage for first-time founders. Should you hire an agency?

The topic of agencies is a tough one. I've found that it's actually more difficult to decide whether to hire an agency than it is to hire your first team members. I think it's because, by definition, you're looking to hire an agency that's going to know more than you do about what you're even hiring them for—and arguably they can do the job better than you can. When you're throwing around the idea of hiring an agency, it usually means you've tapped the max capacity in a certain discipline and can't continue to scale without help, or you want to try something new and don't currently have the skills or resources to do it in-house. Agencies knowing more about their specific area than you do is both a good thing and a bad thing. The whole point of hiring an agency is because they know more than you do, so on the upside you will have a team of professionals who have the skill sets to get the job done. But there are a few downsides you need to be aware of, and as with most tools and strategies available to first-time founders, there's no right or wrong answer—it's all about timing. What does your business need at that current point in time?

Starting with the first principles of building a relationship with an agency, the riskiest challenge and most important foundation to address in the relationship is going to be alignment. Regardless of how well you set up the partnership for success, when push comes to shove, agencies will *always* prioritize doing what's best for them as opposed to doing what is best for you. That's not to sound negative; it's important to understand they're not doing it to slight you or because they're bad people. They're running a business just like you are, they are founders just like you, so just like you, they're going to make sure that the best interests of their business are being met.

> Regardless of how well you set up the partnership for success, when push comes to shove, agencies will *always* prioritize doing what's best for them as opposed to doing what is best for you.

Agencies focused on retaining clients long term are more open to discussing alignment because they realize that having clients stick around and keep paying as long as possible is usually more effective than churning and burning clients. But unfortunately, from my own experience and from hearing the common challenges first-time founders face when dealing with agencies, there are a lot of them that still focus on bringing in new contracts rather than focusing on retaining clients. So instead of blaming agencies for putting themselves first, it's more important to just understand that this is the case, and to take ownership and responsibility for the success of the partnership yourself. Luckily, there are a few things that you're able to do to tip the scales.

I'm going to focus mostly on marketing agencies as examples because I've found this is usually where first-time founders start and where they struggle the most. But these tips can work with all agencies. There are four things that you need to take responsibility for if you want a chance at a successful relationship: alignment, accountability, knowledge, and expectations.

Alignment—Negotiate the Contract

Alignment is simple when it comes to an agency relationship. It looks like this: you get what you need in terms of performance, and the agency gets to retain you as a consistent client and source of income for as long as possible. No need to overcomplicate it. As long as you're getting the results you want, you're happy to pay them for as long as they provide the results.

I've found that contract negotiations boil down to three main components. These vary highly from agency to agency and tend to be very negotiable if done properly:

1. Length of contract
2. Compensation
3. Touch points

First is the length of the contract, or commitment. To avoid any misalignment around paying for a service that you're not receiving— meaning you're paying for a certain level of performance, you're okay with paying for that level of performance, but you're not receiving that performance—it's important to negotiate the length of the contract. I've found that most agencies like to start with six- or twelve-month contracts, which to me is a red flag. I'd recommend negotiating down to three months if possible, using the easy argument: "How can anyone expect someone to sign a yearlong contract when we haven't even seen whether you're capable of doing the job? We're more than happy to extend the contract if we hit these specific milestones that we can agree upon together." This way, your agency will be more incentivized to perform early on with the goal of extending the contract, and therefore you'll be more closely aligned for the campaigns to perform. I like using lines like these because they're based in logic. If you get hard pushback when you're willing to sign extensions as long as you see performance, and you're being pressured into signing something long term without any sort of assurances, that's a concern.

Next is compensation. It's important to note that it's normal and acceptable for any agency to ask for a base monthly fee. However, there are usually some sort of bonus structures added, and these usually involve some sort of rev share, profit share, or commission and are usually structured around a percentage of ad spend, which is a big red flag for me. If an agency is being compensated on percentage of ad spend, what's stopping them from ramping up the ad spend without putting in the real work of optimizing your cost per acquisition (CPA) as well? I won't dive deep into the relationship between CPA and ad spend here, but with that being said, it's important to know that ad spend without CPA management is a recipe for low accountability and wasteful spending. Anybody can see a good CPA with an ad spend of $5,000. Anybody can increase their ad spend from $5,000 to $20,000. But increasing your ad spend from $5,000 to $20,000 while maintaining the same CPA is an art. If you raise your ad spend but your CPA rises to unacceptable levels along with it, you're not scaling—you're just spending more money to get fewer customers.

A way to negotiate the ad spend component of a contract is to create a "CPA cap" and add a performance bonus attached to that. If our current CPA is $50 with a $5,000/month budget, we'll allow you to spend up to $10,000/month; however, the highest we're willing to go on CPA is now $65 (the CPA cap). What you can say is that if you both agree on a CPA cap of $65, then at the end of the month, if the CPA is under $65, they can keep the difference per sale.

A quick example would be if they spend $10,000 in the month and get an overall CPA of $60, which would be 166 sales (total ad spend of $10,000 divided by the CPA of $60), the CPA of $60 is lower than the agreed upon $65 CPA cap, which means that the bonus or commission the agency would get is the difference of the $5 per sale, leaving them with a bonus of $833 (the number of sales, which is 166 times the difference between the actual CPA of $60 and the CPA cap of $65, which is $5). This is a fair way to give the agency the freedom to raise the ad spend but also make sure that they're not doing so if they don't feel they can maintain a reasonable CPA. However, on the other hand, if you raise our ad spend but the CPA goes over $65, then you don't receive any bonus or commission because it means you're not scaling the ads properly. This can be used to create shared alignment, as long as the numbers are agreed upon mutually.

Lastly, something else to bring up early on during the negotiations is weekly or bimonthly touch points. I'll get to this in the next tip, but agreeing upon a certain standard of accountability will not only keep you involved as you should, but it will also let the agency know that you're going to be playing a role in monitoring the account to make sure it has the best possible chances for success.

Banging out these conversations early on will help you with agency alignment. But here's the next challenge: accountability.

Just because you're giving the relationship a small leg up by finding alignment doesn't mean that things are going to go smoothly. You've just hired an agency, which is pretty much the same as bringing on a new employee. There's a responsibility for them to perform, but like every other aspect of your business, the real responsibility of their success lies with you.

Accountability—Never Set It and Forget It

This is one of the biggest issues that first-time founders face when they choose to go with an agency. Because they see bringing on an agency as someone else now handling a particular department or issue, they tend to abdicate responsibility and essentially check out.

I see it all the time. A first-time founder decides to hire a marketing agency because they don't know how to create Facebook ads, or craft creative content, or leverage Google AdWords, or build an audience. And they're of the mindset that once they have the professionals working on it, they can tune out, not follow up, and just wait for their monthly report.

> **As the leader of your organization, how dare you give whatever ungodly amount of money to an agency and not supervise these people!**

I need to call this out: As the leader of your organization, how dare you give whatever ungodly amount of money to an agency and not supervise these people!

Especially when you are incapable of determining whether they're doing a good job or not at the end of the month because they're going to use a bunch of words you don't understand. To me, that's just plain laziness. If you want to succeed, you can't leave any aspect of your business unsupervised—there's no difference with agencies. If you're paying them, you have to monitor them. Period. That's why I always advocate for weekly or bimonthly meetings with your agency.

As you can probably imagine, the agency is going to push back and claim it's unnecessary or that it's not how these types of relationships work. That's a red flag, because there is no good reason a decent agency wouldn't be willing to meet with you to give you peace of mind. It's not about being unreasonable and demanding that the agency be at your beck and call so you can micromanage them and distract them from their day to day, but a quick fifteen- to thirty-minute touch point should be acceptable and understandable.

Typically, agencies will push back because they're not planning on dedicating the time, it's too much of a headache, or they don't want to be held accountable to give you weekly updates because they're worried you might find holes. You'll hear things like, "Well, it takes a few months to ramp up," or "There won't be a lot of progress in the first few months while we're diving in," or "It's all implementation for us right now." Some of these things are definitely true, but don't buy into an agency that says things like that as an excuse not to have a touch point. At the end of the day, your company is likely one of dozens they are contracted to help. They are never going to care as much or be as invested in your business as you and your team. So there is nothing wrong with holding accountability by staying top of mind in a respectful and productive way.

I've told this to first-time founders for a long time now, and I was surprised at how many of them thought that it was weird to keep an eye on their agencies in the early days. What was more interesting was some of the excuses that people would give as to why they felt they couldn't be responsible for managing their agency in this way. It was usually things like, "How can I meet with them if I don't know anything about what they do?" This leads me to my next tip.

Knowledge—Become Familiar with the Agency's Discipline

I started this chapter by saying that the success of the partnership is your responsibility, and I meant that. At the end of the day, if an agency doesn't work out, you can blame the agency all you want, but it's still your loss. Regardless of whose fault it is, you're the one who lost out on the time, money, and energy. And as I've mentioned earlier in the book, it's important to understand that even if it is someone else's fault, if there is a chance to make it work, it's your job to make it work.

This leads us to knowledge. As discussed previously, you must hold your agency accountable, which means you must have your follow-up calls. It also means you must at very minimum be able to have a high-level conversation about what they're doing, how they're doing it, and whether or not it's working. You need to at least become *familiar* with whatever discipline the agency specializes in. You don't have to know the ins and outs of how to use Facebook Business Manager or how to dive into Google Analytics, or anything like that. But you better be able to understand questions around, let's say, cost per acquisition and why it may or may not be working. If you're dealing with a development agency, you better be able to understand why they're using a specific programming language. You don't have to know the language. You don't have to know how it works. You don't have to suddenly learn how to code. But you better be able to understand the pros and cons of the system they're suggesting. I know this might sound daunting to some first-time founders, but there's no other way to say it other than it's your responsibility, and you have to do it if you want a successful relationship.

Now this is where it all comes together. If you can honestly look yourself in the mirror and say you've done a good job of finding alignment early on, you're following through with accountability, and you have a basic high-level knowledge of what you've hired them to do, now is when you get to set the expectations for the agency.

Expectations—Don't Let the Agency Blame You for Their Failures

This tip only works if you've done the previous tips. If you just skip to this rule without doing the previous work, then there's a good chance that you're just making excuses, and there's more that could have been done to make the relationship a success. But if you've done the work, here's where you get to push back.

What I see all the time, particularly with marketing agencies, is they promise you the sun, the world, the moon, and the stars. They can quadruple your revenue in less than six months and even reduce your cost per acquisition while doing it. Then what happens is, five months down the line, you're in a situation where—surprise, surprise—things aren't working out like they said they would, and now they say something like, "Listen, we weren't able to do as well as expected. The ads aren't performing the way we thought they would."

To be honest, I can live with that. If I did everything in my power for it to be successful, and I felt the agency did the same, I can live with a failure. But the part that I would find really frustrating was their reasoning. It also became more apparent that this wasn't an isolated incident, seeing as almost every founder I'd consult would mention a similar experience at one time or another. Instead of taking responsibility and saying they bit off more than they could chew, or they underestimated the challenges in your industry, or just overall that they overpromised and underdelivered, they'll say things like, "We weren't able to get the results we promised because your content wasn't good enough," or "Your pictures aren't in the right format," or "Your videos aren't engaging or targeted enough," and lastly, "Your website doesn't convert properly." They will shower you with a million and one excuses as to why they can't perform.

Now, they may very well be right. If any part of a campaign is off, then the overall campaign has a low chance of success. After all, marketing is broken up into two distinct and separate elements: content and distribution. Founders love to focus on the distribution by funneling marketing dollars into Facebook, Google, or affiliate networks but often neglect the content that is being distributed. However, the issue here is that *they* (the agency) are the marketing experts. *They* know what it takes to be successful. *They* are the ones making the commitment to performance. If they knew there were roadblocks like poor content, it's my opinion that they should be flagging these roadblocks in advance, either during the contract negotiation or right after the preliminary dive-in. For this reason, I feel it's important to push back if these are the excuses that have been used as to why your campaign didn't perform.

To help avoid these situations, if you hire an agency, make sure you ask them to clearly identify any potential roadblocks to success. A good marketing agency will call out bad content right away and work to get that up to par before launching any kind of campaign, or at the very least give you a direction to go in terms of getting your content to where it needs to be before beginning.

I left this tip as the last one for a specific reason. I mentioned it early in the chapter, but if the partnership fails, regardless of who's fault it is, you and your business suffer the most. So I find it important to use this tip last because it forces you to do as much as possible to set things up for success from the get-go. This isn't unique to marketing agencies. And in the example of a development agency, make sure they're fully scoping out the project or your existing systems to make sure that, midway through, they don't come back and use unannounced roadblocks as ways to increase the cost of the project.

Like a lot of tools and strategies, it's not necessarily right or wrong to use an agency. It's more of a function of what your business needs at that point in time. There is a time and place to hire an agency. They all serve different purposes at different times. With truLOCAL, we went to marketing agencies when we didn't have the skill sets in-house. And when we brought the skill sets in-house, we ended the arrangements with the agencies. Then when a new marketing channel came up for which we lacked the skills and knowledge, we went back to the agency. Think of agencies as filling a temporary gap until you grow to the point where you can move on or, if it makes sense, bring the skill set in-house.

Choosing the right agency is hard, especially if you're not an expert in the field. But an agency relationship that is set up properly from the beginning can supercharge your business and give you a competitive advantage against your competitors. Working with agencies is a necessary step as a first-time founder. But it's a lot like driving a purpose-built race car. No traction control, 550 horsepower, rear-wheel drive—it can be an experience that changes your world for the better—*if* you know how to manage it. If not, you're going to crash and burn. That doesn't make the car bad. It means you were an irresponsible driver.

It's the same with agencies. They serve a great purpose; they can change your business for the better. Agencies allow you to move significantly faster while tapping into professional resources. The only thing is you better be competent enough to manage that agency, so you don't crash and burn.

PART III

All That Matters Is Putting in the Work

CHAPTER NINE

Raising Capital with Angels and Venture Capitalists

Chase the vision, not the money; the money will end up following you.

—TONY HSIEH, ZAPPOS CEO

All right, so the time is finally here. You and your cofounder have reached the point where you need to raise money to get to the next level. You've heard the saying before: *it takes money to make money.* But it's important to note that not all money is the same. It might not feel this way, but please trust me when I say, *raising money isn't the hard part.* Raising the right kind of money from the right people is the hard part. There are a ton of options when it comes to raising capital: friends, family, angel investors, venture capitalists, and bank loans and equity crowdfunding, just to name a few.

> Raising money isn't the hard part. Raising the right kind of money from the right people is the hard part.

So with all these options, how do you know which is the right choice for your business? In this chapter I want to give a high-level overview of some key things to note when you're thinking about raising money from investors for the first time. There are no rules for this; raising money is the Wild West. Yes, there are best practices that can help give you a framework to follow, but some of the biggest closes have come from outside-of-the-box thinking. With that being said, I hope this serves as a general overview.

It doesn't matter where you are in your start-up. Guaranteed pitching for a check isn't just something that you've thought about; it's probably something you've fantasized about. This is a big moment for first-time founders. You've probably been told it's a rite of passage. Typically, first-time founders fall into one of two camps—over the top excited, or cripplingly anxious.

But regardless, raising money is a bridge most first-time founders are going to cross. So knowing that, it's important to know that, as with most things, knowledge is power. The more you understand about the various rounds of financing and how they work, the better prepared you'll be and the more likely you'll be to secure a deal that's right for you.

So first, let's get to know the players.

The Players

The two major players that you'll probably be dealing with when it comes to raising your first round are angel investors and venture capitalists (VCs). You've probably heard these terms before, but what they don't teach you in start-up school is there's a very big difference between the two. To put it plainly, angel investors are high-net-worth individuals who are willing to invest their money. They want to sprinkle their wealth and invest either in a person who they feel a connection to, want to mentor, or just believe in. Or they want exposure to an industry where they personally see opportunity. Either way, angel investors tend to invest more with their gut rather than with a team of analysts. Most of the angels you'll interact with are probably just investing on their own, so one of the good things about angels is they tend to have very light contracts. What I mean by that is you're not going to have to go through a whole panel of analysts and a bombardment of lawyers to draft and review investment paperwork. More likely than not, it's going to be a very simple and very short document—maybe a brief term sheet to highlight the specifics of the deal, followed by closing documents. This is for a couple of reasons: (1) usually angels tend to be a little more founder friendly and understand that for their investment to be protected, you as the founding team need to be happy and safe; and (2) sometimes they just aren't interested in doing a full round of due diligence, they don't necessarily even want to negotiate every single aspect of a deal, or they're happy with standard clauses and just want to see you start putting the money to work.

With that being said, it is important to note that, depending on how you set up the deal with your lawyers, they do have an entitlement to see your financials and probe about how things are going. This is fine unless you end up with a micromanager. I've seen it happen before where an angel will put in a small amount of money, maybe like $25,000 for 2.5 percent, and the next thing you know they are in the founder's office every day asking for reports. If an angel is nervous and watching every single dime like a hawk, it could be a sign that they may have spread themselves too thin on this investment. If an angel doesn't have cash they are willing to lose, you shouldn't take money from them in the first place. Piggy backing on some of the previous chapters, and you might have already guessed it, but this can be easily avoided by clearly outlining and discussing expectations.

My experience has been with silent angels. A lot of founders at this stage know what they want. They already know where they need to go.

They really just need the money to get their products off the ground or start hiring. So, most of the time, having a silent angel is pretty nice. A silent angel just means someone who is going to give you the money and trust you to execute. They're not interested in taking part in the day-to-day operations or being actively involved with requests or suggestions. They'll check in once a quarter, and you send them the financials, but they believe in you to do what's the best for the business.

On the other hand though, if you have a very complex business that requires a lot of R&D and insider knowledge, let's say an enterprise software company specializing in cyber security as an example, then maybe you want an angel who can bring a little bit more than just money to the table. Maybe you want to go for someone with a little more experience who can open doors and walk you into meetings. There are a lot of angels who fit this description, but this also leads us to VCs.

At their core, VCs are professional investors usually organized as a firm. They typically have larger teams made up of analysts who vet out the market in search of businesses to invest in; general partners (GPs) who manage the firm and, for the most part, call the shots and decide which companies to invest in; and limited partners (LPs), who are the individuals or organizations investing their money into the fund so that the firm can go make investments. Usually as a rule of thumb, VCs have specific industries they'll focus on or rounds they prefer to take part in. But I do want to quickly highlight again that this is a generalization, there are definitely also VCs that play in all industries and all rounds.

Now, VCs can be great. However, it's important to understand that VCs are in the business of turning a profit for their investors. A VC might have a portfolio of different companies, and you can be sure that they're going to spend most of their time and focus on the companies that are doing the best. VCs also hold the investment thesis that nine out of ten of their investments are going to fail. They spread their investments in the hope that one of them becomes a money tree.

This was really interesting to me because I remember pitching VCs back in the day and saying, "Listen, we can get you 3X or 4X on your money." And it always used to blow my mind when the VCs would shrug it off. I honestly couldn't understand how, if I was pitching to someone that we could quadruple their investment, they would be looking at that as a failure. But once you really understand the VC thesis where most of their investments are going to zero, it starts to make more sense that 3X or 4X doesn't help them. They want a home run. They *need* a home run. If their fund has a ten-year horizon, meaning that after ten years, they need to return the money to their investors (the LPs), and they know that most of their investments are going to fail, they need to have a few 10X plays to ensure that their investors see returns. So when they evaluate your start-up, the question for them is "Can you be a home run?"

It's also important to punch in your weight class. The size of a VC's fund plays a huge role in whether you're going to be a good fit for them or not. You'll have a hard time going to a $500 million fund trying to raise $50,000. Why? You're probably thinking that $50,000 is nothing to a big firm like that—just shoot a couple pennies my way! It's worth the risk. But think about it: even if you end up being a home run, you overperform the market and do everything you promise. If you're a breakout success and you 10X your business, that investment of $50,000 only ends up being $500,000 payout to the firm. To a $500 million fund, that's *0.1 percent*. In the eyes of a VC, it's not worth getting out of bed considering the stats that they're more likely to lose that whole investment let alone make their money back or get a 10X. Make sure to target VCs whose fund size is proportionate to the amount you're looking to raise. Things that could make a difference here are if you're a hot start-up, or the VC wants to take a chance on you, there are some VCs who will take part in rounds that are smaller than usual with the mindset that they'll take a small position now to make sure they have their foot in the door should things pop off. The excitement here for the VC is the opportunity to take a larger position later on or even lead the next round.

With VCs, you're going to get professional-level support. You're going to get access to accountants and lawyers and to networks that you would have had a hard time accessing without them. On the other hand, VCs are always going to have heavy-handed contracts, will enforce governance that you won't be used to, and will almost always structure the deal in their benefit. They are going to have things like liquidation preferences—meaning if you go under, they get paid first. Preferred shares mean that they have special voting rights, and more likely than not they're going to want board seats. These are all things you really need to consider when thinking about bringing on a VC. Do the pros outweigh the cons? A lot of the time they do. It's very industry specific. If you're in a service-based business, or a company where you're more focused on profits rather than growth, VC money might not be the best option. But if you're in a high-tech R&D, if you're in cyber security, if you're in enterprise software solutions, or if you're in a winner-take-all market, then it's very much a "Who do you know?" and "How fast can you grow?" game, and VCs

> Just remember that there's nothing more valuable than equity, and unless there's a strategic reason to rush financing, try to build the value of your equity for as long as possible before raising any capital.

can play a very big role. So it's very important to understand what type of business you have before deciding whether or not you want to go down the VC road.

One other factor to understand with VCs is if you have the idea of potentially selling one day or being acquired, your VC may put a lot of roadblocks in place if you get offers that they're not happy with. If you go ahead and get a million dollars from a VC, and you go and triple the size of the business in a year, then someone offers you triple the amount for the business, that's great for you. It's not good for the VC.

VCs are a good option. You just need to understand what they're good for. Regardless of angels or VCs, just remember that there's nothing more valuable than equity, and unless there's a strategic reason to rush financing, try to build the value of your equity for as long as possible before raising any capital.

Knowing the Rounds

Traditionally, fundraising rounds are labeled with different names. Now, the thing to note here is that recently these rounds have really started to blend and blur together. Back in the day, fundraising rounds were more formal and had very specific milestones or raise amounts. First, you would do your friends-and-family round. Then you would do an angel round. Then you would do a seed round. And then you could do your series A round, then series B round, etc.

In all these rounds, you were typically getting a certain ceiling of dollars. So if you were going for X amount of money, you were probably in round X. Or if you've done two of these rounds before and you're looking for X amount of money, you're now in round Y. You used to see $5 million to $10 million checks only come out of series A rounds. But now you're starting to see the dollar amounts shift a little bit to what was previously considered earlier rounds. It's not uncommon to see larger check sizes being written in the seed rounds.

The bottom line is the names of these rounds aren't as important as they used to be. They are more or less used to give everyone a framework of what investors are looking for.

ROUND	WHO TO GO TO	HOW MUCH YOU CAN RAISE	WHAT THEY'RE LOOKING FOR
(GENERAL RULE OF THUMB)			
Friends and family round	Friends and family who have disposable income and believe in you	This depends on family and friends <$50,000	A hope and a prayer that you won't lose all their money
Angel round	Wealthy individuals known as angels	$50,000 to $500,000	Looking at • Founders
Seed round	Angels and certain early-stage VCs	$250,000 to $5,000,000	Looking at • The product/ service • To achieve product market fit • Signs of early traction
Series A and beyond	VCs	$5,000,000+	Looking at • Metrics • Scalability • Market opportunity

THE FRIENDS-AND-FAMILY ROUND

This round is typically going to be your first round and is exactly what it sounds like. You're pretty much asking your friends and family to invest in you. You're probably not even giving them a supersophisticated pitch. You're just saying, "Hey, listen, I've got this idea. Would you be willing to fund me?"

Personally, I've never loved the idea of doing a friends-and-family round, because despite being a huge proponent for hiring friends, taking money from friends and family can be sticky. First of all, it's a little bit too easy. These people care about you and aren't likely to vet you or your idea the same way a more sophisticated investor might. You may get the start-up capital you need, but mostly because these people want to support your dreams, not because your business model is sound. It may be low-hanging fruit, which is nice if you have access to it, but there is a special perspective that can only come from the rite of passage of being grilled by investors. Despite how frustrating that process can be, hearing "no" a lot will help you refine your idea, tweak your business model, and help you spot pitfalls you may not have noticed otherwise. If you only go straight to the easy "yes" people in your life, you may miss out on valuable critiques that could improve your chances of success.

THE ANGEL ROUND—FOCUSING ON THE FOUNDER

This round is named after the typical players in the space, which are angel investors. This round is a first-time founder's first serious investor who will judge you based on the merits of your business and on your ability to execute. But more so than anything else, this round tends to be mainly about selling yourself as a founder. It's about making sure you build a relationship with the individual, while also making sure that the market opportunity lines up with what they're interested in. Generally speaking, an angel's knowledge tends to be on a specific market rather than a broad range. A lot of them are just wealthy individuals who have made their money in alternative spaces and are interested in investing and supporting early-stage founders. So the main focus for them is going to be learning who you are as a founder.

Nowadays, you'll probably approach a single angel investor for anything from $5,000 to $250,000 with the whole idea of this round being focused on getting you and your business off the X.

THE SEED ROUND—FOCUSING ON THE PRODUCT AND THE EARLY TRACTION

So you've got a business plan, and you've shown that there's a market opportunity. Just like it sounds, this is the round focused on seeding your business with the hopes of getting your product or service to market. Your seed round is also where you might start to see a little bit of an overlap between choosing angels or VCs.

My personal preference is going with angels versus VCs in this round, just because they're not going to give you the same strings attached in your contracts, and you can get the same amount of money. Typically in a seed round, a good rule of thumb is going for $500,000 to $2 million. But once again, even these numbers are changing dramatically.

The thing that investors are looking for during this round is focused on product. What exactly is the product or service? How does it work? And have you been able to prove that there's a need? Is there a measurable interest around your solution? As investors, if you're planning on using this money to bring a product to life, they'll will want to see some sort of market research. They want to see an audience. They want to see purchase orders ready to go. They want to see contracts signed for when the product is ready. Even without the full expression of your product being live yet, they want to see that there is a buzz from your potential customers. You can have the best business plan in the world, but if you can't prove a need, you won't close this round. The goal for the money you raise during your seed round should focus around achieving a term you've probably heard thrown around before called "product market fit." This just means that after various rounds of iteration, you've proven that the product you've built solves a specific problem for your audience, and you'll be able to tell if you have product market fit if your business is starting to see a measurable uptick in adoption.

SERIES A ROUND AND BEYOND—FOCUSING ON THE METRICS AND SCALABILITY

This round is where things get serious. These rounds are aptly named because they typically come in a series (A, B, C, D, etc.) that represent various stages. Series A round financing is traditionally done with VCs. A venture capital firm will come in as your lead investor to take a point on the deal, which pretty much just means they're signalling to the market that they're funding you, and that they'll help by making connections to other VCs or confirming to investors that they will be taking part in the round. The lead VC typically also sets the terms for the deal. From there, you can then fill up the round with other venture capitalists or even angels if the VC is open to it.

During these rounds, investors are laser focused on your metrics. You've already got a product, it's out in the market, and you've proven you're growing. What they want to know is if you have healthy metrics based on your industry so that you can start doubling down and injecting capital to scale the business. There's a good chance that investors in this round might already have an idea of *yes* or *no* before even meeting you because they just need to look at the numbers to see what's going on.

You Have Your Investor. Now What?

Now, you've found your angel or VC and it's time to write the check. So how does that actually work?

Traditional financing is most common for first-time founders in the early stages. This is known as equity financing. So let's say an angel puts money into your business, and the business issues shares to the angel. People who watch shows like *Dragons' Den* and *Shark Tank* hear stuff like, "I'll give you $100,000 for 20 percent of your business." And everybody thinks that means the investor bought 20 percent from the founders, leaving them with 80 percent. That's not how it works in real life. When you're doing an equity financing round, the investor is not buying shares from any individual—they are getting shares issued to them from the treasury of the business. It's very important to understand that, because the main difference is that, when someone is investing, you are not selling your already-owned shares; otherwise you'd be the one receiving the money, not the business. What's happening is the business is issuing new shares to give to the new investor, hence why the capital goes to the business. Early on this took me a really long time to understand, but it's important that you work with a good lawyer who can walk you through this when the time comes.

So how do you figure out what your company is actually worth? That's called your valuation. Note the word is not *evaluation*. You say *evaluation* to an investor, and the deal is over. It's the *valuation* of the business. It's important to understand this, because this is what dictates how much equity the investor will get for their investment.

There are a million and one different ways to come up with valuations. But the problem that most small first-time founders deal with is within your first year you don't have a significant customer base or consistent revenue. You maybe have a year's worth of data. At such an early stage, you aren't necessarily in a position to set a valuation, and neither is the investor.

So to get around this dilemma, investors use something called a convertible note, or a convertible debt. This is the most common way for people to get their first round of financing. What this would look like is the investor agrees to invest $100,000, then based on a certain trigger—it could be a time, it could be a dollar milestone, it could be when you do your next round—the investor is going to convert that $100,000 loan into equity in your business when the valuation is decided later on. Or they can keep it as a loan.

Not a lot of first-time founders love convertible notes because they may be stuck with the liability of having a loan to repay in cash. What happened commonly as a result was all these investors were muscling small founders into shitty deals. Then, as they started seeing some success and the value of the business went through the roof, these silent investors ended up with a disproportionately high number of shares—or equity—in the business, compared to the value they were providing.

In order to address this, Y-Combinator, a prominent silicon valley accelerator, came up with something called a SAFE—simple agreement for future equity. A SAFE is similar to a convertible note, except you don't have the liability of having to repay it in cash; it's always going to be converted to equity. The SAFE is set up to automatically execute on the following round of funding.

The realization was that instead of an investor being able to milk every last drop out of a deal, it actually makes more sense to have founder-friendly deals, so the founders are motivated to keep growing the business and win. An example of the idea of a SAFE is "I'm going to give you $100,000. We're not going to talk about valuation. Instead, keep growing the business, and when you do your next round, my money will convert at the time when the institutional investor comes in." Because at the end of the day, it's the VCs who can provide a more accurate valuation of the business.

A SAFE is pretty straightforward. The only thing you're negotiating is the *discount* and the *cap*. The discount is standard at 20 percent, meaning that because they're coming in early and not getting as sweet of a deal as they would if it was a convertible note, they'll get a 20 percent discount on the shares they're buying. Essentially, if they put in $100,000, they'll get $120,000 worth of shares. The discount helps to sweeten the pot for early investors, however the cap is usually the most negotiated part of a SAFE. The cap is the highest valuation that the investor's money will convert at, regardless of the actual valuation of the next financing round. Let's look at an example of why a cap is important. Say an investor gives you $100,000 and things are rocking and rolling in the business, and you don't end up needing to raise money for five years. When you do go and raise money, you raise at a $50 million valuation, well that $100,000 isn't going to be worth a whole lot anymore, and the investor has now missed out on all of that upside. Founder-friendly deals are good, but there still needs to be protection for the investor.

When you incorporate the "cap," the example would look like this: Say you sign a SAFE with an investor and you have a $8 million cap (at the time of writing, $8 million is a standard), then you see a string of wins, so when you raise your next round you realize that you're going to raise at a $50 million valuation. Regardless of the $50 million valuation, because the SAFE has a $8 million cap, the SAFE investors' money will convert at the $8 million.

It's a great mechanism, because investors can't gouge these early-stage founders, but on the other hand the founders have the ability to grow their businesses and get a proper valuation while keeping the investors protected.

So Where Do I Find Angels and VCs?

So where do you start? The friends-and-family thing is easy if you want to go that route. You know where to find them. But how do you find angels and VCs? Well, go where the rich people are. Finesse your way into some sort of conference, check out an investor or angel event on meetup.com, or walk into a VC office and bug an analyst. Once you're at these places, talk. A lot. Talk to as many people as possible because one day you will find someone who's interested in what you're doing.

You may not know rich people directly, but you might at least know people who know people who have money. Just be honest and ask them, "Can I get your feedback on something I'm working on?" Don't even expect to get funding, but use it as an opportunity to ask them for another introduction. When you know one rich person, they will make intro-ductions to other rich people. They typically love to talk and love to share contacts, so don't hesitate to connect.

> VCs are always willing to take meetings. They *want* to sit with founders, especially if you're in their industry.

In addition to that, there are angel networks. Most cities have some sort of investor network, so check out the angel investment networks in your own city. Make it a point to attend any and all meetings. The same philosophy applies to VCs. You need to get out there and start pitching. VCs are always willing to take meetings. They *want* to sit with founders, especially if you're in their industry.

A few final tips for working with investors are listed below.

INVESTOR TIP 1: INVESTORS WANT TO INVEST

You need to realize that when you ask investors for money, you are not bothering them. That's the number one thing that helped my mindset. When you start to realize that every single person saying yes to a pitch meeting is begging for you to pitch them the next Google and that they're actively hoping to find a founder to invest their money into, you understand that it's your meeting to lose.

INVESTOR TIP 2: IF YOU WANT MONEY, ASK FOR HELP. IF YOU WANT HELP, ASK FOR MONEY.

If you're having trouble getting meetings, or if you're having trouble building those relationships with angels or VCs, remember this: "If you want money, ask for help. If you want help, ask for money." If you just come out point-blank and say, "Hey, do you want to invest in me?" it's probably not going to work out very well. You need to build that relationship. And the only way to build a relationship in the right way is to let someone know who you are.

If you immediately come out and ask for money, it's hard to have that candid, get-to-know-me sort of conversation. Instead, if you ask for help, rich people are always down to help, and VCs are down to help as well. Now, you get to spend some time with them. They can see how you think, and they can see what you're all about. You can spend more time building relationships, and then eventually just by them helping you, they're going to get a better understanding of the business and might become interested in investing.

And as a final word on raising money as a first-time founder: don't buy into the myth that success is gauged by how much money you raise. Just because you raised $2 million doesn't mean you crossed the finish line. Sure, you can pat yourself on the back. But raising money means there is even more work to do. And the more you raise, the more work you create.

As soon as you take money from people, you now have to be accountable to these individuals, which isn't necessarily a bad thing. But raising money just for the sake of raising money isn't winning. So if you can avoid raising money, do it. Money doesn't make your business better. It doesn't make your business stronger. It doesn't make you smarter. All money does is allow you to move faster. That's it.

And despite how important speed is to your business, ownership and equity retention are more important in the long run. So if you're able to keep equity, do it. If you can go on for a long time without raising money, do it.

CHAPTER TEN

Building Community by Finding Your Own Niche

He who masters the power formed by a group of people working together has within his grasp one of the greatest powers known to man.

—IDOWU KOYENIKAN

Despite all the different industries and all the variations of businesses within those industries, at the end of the day, every single business has one thing in common: they all require you to build a customer base. But more importantly, you need to realize that your customers—both paying and nonpaying—are your *community*.

If you want to run a successful business, you'll need to get past simply looking at customer acquisition strategies and start focusing on community building as well. Having a strong community will not only make it easier to acquire customers, but it will also improve the perception of your brand, make it easier to acquire and retain top talent, and provide you with a competitive advantage against other players in your industry that don't have their own community. As a side note, this is becoming even more important as Web3 continues its mainstream adoption. Digital memberships in the form of NFTs, and online communities managing shared bank accounts called DAOs, are at their core highly aligned and functional communities.

Back in the day, businesses may have gotten away with providing the bare minimum: "Here's our offering. You pay us for our offering. Be happy; you got what you paid for." But in my opinion, providing what was marketed is a default. If you market a product or service, your job, at the very least, is to provide that product or service, but today that's not enough. More likely than not, consumers can get that same product or service somewhere else, especially if you're in a highly competitive space like any D2C brand currently is. If you're just providing the bare minimum service, you are *extracting* value from your customers. However, looking at your customer base as a community instead of just paying customers is how you can get away from the idea of purely extracting value, and instead understanding that your customers are worth much more than the dollar value you can make off them. It's *your* job to nurture that. This takes customer management from extraction to nurture.

> If you market a product or service, your job, at the very least, is to provide that product or service, but today that's not enough.

In addition to switching from extraction to nurture, community building also addresses a facet of building that keeps people loyal for the long term. There needs to be a sense of belonging, a sense of why people want to buy your product or service. Outside of your core offering, that's what makes a company unique. And that's why you need to understand what community really means. Community building is one of the single most important weapons in your arsenal when it comes to retaining customers when a new competitor pops up. A strong community is what will prevent customers from leaving you, even if a competitor launches with a slightly better or cheaper offering.

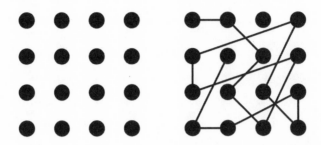

So how do you build a community? What is a community? Where does that even come from?

In my eyes, a community is simply a group of people who unite around a shared passion, a shared goal, a shared alignment, a shared love of *something*. And the way you get people to start feeling that sense of attachment is through a strong brand.

People talk about how branding is everything. If you are wondering if that's true, the answer is it's *half true*. Branding is everything. However, the other half of that equation is that if you're able to come up with a great brand, your job is then to make sure that every single aspect of your business, from the product you offer, to the experience of your website, to the content in your ads, to the way your consumer experience team interacts with customers—*everything*—lives up to this image you've created with your brand. Your brand is a promise, and it's your job and your team's job to live up to that promise. Anybody can come up with a cool logo or color scheme, or hire an agency to come up with a branding package. From there, *some* people are able to attach a

> Your brand is a promise, and it's your job and your team's job to live up to that promise.

really strong mission to that or tap into a movement that gets people excited. However, only a small group of businesses can then ensure that the company lives up to "promises" made by the brand image. While I was at truLOCAL, that was one of the main things we wanted to prove—to emphasize that with a strong brand, and a focus on ensuring that our business lived up to that brand, any business can be successful. If we could use branding and community building to make *meat* relatable, Instagrammable, and cool, any business can do it.

So where do you start? Well, first and most importantly is understanding what a brand even is. If you ask the most talented marketing expert, "What exactly is a brand?" they will likely go into some long-winded answer that leaves you with more questions than answers by the end of it. For me, explaining a brand is simple: a brand is how people feel when they think about your company.

If you think about Lululemon, McDonald's, Nike, Apple, Tesla, or Coinbase, as soon as you hear one of those names or see that logo, you get a feeling—it could be a sense of happiness, or joy, or cheekiness. It could be a sense of quality or warmth, a sense of comfort, a sense of trust. On the other hand, some brands will immediately give you a sense of dislike, a sense of distaste, a sense of cheap. Regardless of what it is, you get a *feeling*. And that is the essence of a brand. Once people start to feel something before even conceptualizing your business, you've officially established a brand in people's minds.

That kind of brand power isn't something that happens overnight. It's something that is ingrained and reflected in every single action of the business. How people feel when they think about a brand is a culmination of all the big things a company does and all the small things a company does.

So now that you understand what a brand is, where's the starting point for using that brand to create a community?

Start Niche

Start by finding a niche. Everybody wants to start with mainstream, and everybody wants to be everything to everybody. If you look at most first-time founder pitch decks, so many times they think they're doing themselves a favor by saying, "We cater to the twenty-five-year-old all the way to the sixty-five-year-old. Everybody loves us."

This kind of thinking is actually doing you and your business a disservice. Because when you really think about it, very rarely is there a single company that caters to that wide of a demographic. What really happens when you cast a wide net like that is you end up doing nothing for nobody. You end up spending money on content that doesn't resonate with people, and you end up with a product or service that feels like it's missing depth. But most importantly you end up making brand promises to too many people, and by servicing one group of customers, you let your promises slip for the opposite group. When it comes to building a community, you absolutely need to find a niche, then cater toward that niche. You've probably heard the quote: "You're better off finding the first one hundred customers that love you than the thousand that like you." That sentiment couldn't be more true.

Why is that? It's because the power of word of mouth in a niche community is way stronger than in mainstream, because niche communities love their niche communities. If you're in a niche community, it's because you love that thing. And if you like it, you talk about it. Whereas mainstream loves everything, so they don't really have that die-hard mentality. For mainstream, it's whatever the flavor of the week is.

So as the saying goes, instead of coming out with a brand and going after a community where you get ten thousand people who might like you but not love you enough to tell a friend, make a post, or write a review, you'll be better off going after a niche community where one hundred people love you. And believe it or not, you don't need a lot of people to support you in the early days to get your business and community off the ground. You might think you need a thousand followers, or five thousand followers, or ten thousand followers to look like a growing and successful business. But the reality is if you have fifty reviews, that makes you look like a big company. If you have fifty posts on social, you actually look like a company that people want to be a part of.

Conversely, if you go after the mainstream customers, not only are you going to try to get ten thousand people to like you and not love you, but you need to watch what you wish for because you might actually bring them in. And once they get in, they start looking around and realize you have a customer base and maybe some cool marketing and content but no community that is die hard about you. Don't forget, mainstream likes what's "in and cool," and there's nothing that creates this sense of growing relevance or FOMO (fear of missing out) than following a new brand and realizing they already have this hyper-engaged and deep community that you now want to be a part of. However, if those people join and they realize that there's nothing really behind your brand, and it's mostly transient users or members, the mainstream audience will do what mainstream audiences do— eventually lose interest and move on to the next.

Whereas if you go after your niche market, play it small, get your one hundred fans who love you, then tweak and iterate your product, messaging, and brand toward those one hundred fans. Soon enough, you'll get two hundred fans in that niche. Eventually over time, you'll find that you've won over a majority of fans in that niche that nobody else was even going after because you took the time to identify a way for your business to bend to the needs of a small, underserved community that nobody else was catering to. Once you've established yourself, you have the option of doing it all over again with another adjacent niche, doing it properly to make sure that you don't alienate your existing group. If you do it properly, soon you will actually have a thousand customers who love you, which means you've created a community that will work for you just as hard as you work for them. Then and only then, when you've built a community, understand that community, have created buzz within your community, and truly are in tune with the heartbeat of that community, you'll realize that if you keep expanding into more and more niches, eventually you will have reached "the mainstream majority" without ever marketing to them. *That* is what allows you to springboard your success.

With truLOCAL, we did all these things. We created the brand, we focused on living up to the brand, and then we focused on a small community that we could cater to.

In terms of living up to the brand we created, we always looked like we were more established than we were. We looked like we were ahead of the competition. We looked like we were better able to service the needs of our customers. We looked like we were better funded, even though we weren't. Yes, we were punching above our weight class. When people came in the door, they came in the door because of the brand. But as a subscription-based business, having people come in the door isn't enough. We needed to make sure we lived up to the promise the brand made so that we could retain these new customers. So with every interaction, we knew we had to go above and beyond. We needed to make sure that the website experience lived up to the brand that we'd promised them. We needed to make sure the customer interaction, quality of the product, and follow-up service was solid and on brand.

When we felt confident that we were living up to the image we created with our brand, it came time to start nurturing our community. We knew that our customers were forty-five-year-old moms. We knew that we wanted to go after the healthy mother who came home and wanted to feed their families. But that's also what every single food company was going after, and those people wanted to see credibility.

When it came to finding our first niche, we realized early on that our customer base was perfectly aligned with the CrossFit community. After about a year, we ended up noticing that we were getting a lot of customers who heard about us through their friends at various CrossFit gyms. We noticed that if a couple customers came from a specific gym, within the month we'd see a major spike of orders coming from other members of that same gym. Turns out that if someone was a truLOCAL customer at a CrossFit gym and they started talking about us, that word of mouth made other people in the gym want to give us a shot as well. We doubled down on CrossFit, and we leaned into that community for almost a year and a half as our audience. We had found our first niche.

We would do popup shops at CrossFit gyms literally almost every single night. We reached out to every single CrossFit gym in Ontario. We would call them. We would do whatever we needed to do. We'd just go there, cook up some chicken, and stand there for five hours while they were doing classes, just giving out samples. The CrossFit community loved it, and it was a perfect match. It wasn't until we had earned the respect and trust of the community around CrossFit that we started slowly, one by one, branching out to more niche audiences. Over the years this ended up including niches like the keto community in 2018, and the WW (formerly known as Weight Watchers) community in 2019.

Get in tight with a niche community, and word spreads like wildfire. Make a promise with your brand, and if you work like hell to live up to that promise, before you know it you'll have your own community.

CHAPTER ELEVEN

Transitioning as a Founder

It is not the most intellectual or the strongest of species that survives;
but the species that survives is the one that is able to adapt to and adjust best
to the changing environment in which it finds itself.

—CHARLES DARWIN

Self-awareness is just as important in life as it is in business. And one of the things to understand in your later years as a first-time founder is that, even though you won't be and definitely don't need to be the smartest or most talented person in the organization, you do need to be the best version of yourself to lead the vision. If you want to put together a team of heavy hitters, you need to be able to maintain their respect as an operator. This means that some things you should be self-conscious about are your own development, your focus on transitioning as a founder, and doing everything in your power to avoid plateauing as a leader.

> **You should be self-conscious about your own development, your focus on transitioning as a founder, and doing everything in your power to avoid plateauing as a leader.**

Transitioning along with your business as a founder is one of the most important growth aspects of start-ups. You need to transition just as quickly and rapidly as your business, because as your business is growing, the needs of the business are going to grow and change. As the business gets bigger, as the business gets more customers, as it gets more money, as it gets more traction, as it gets more competition, the needs of the leader are going to change and what your team needs from you is also going to change along with it. Your job is to stay at minimum one step ahead.

Typically, these changes are not a function of time. They are more a function of milestones. I truly believe that every business under $15 million to $20 million changes at its core every $2 million in revenue. So what worked when you were making $2 million is not going to work when you're making $4 million. And that is going to fundamentally change when you make $6 million. And the whole business is going to look different by $8 million, and so forth. But the milestone that induces change in the business might not be tied to revenue. It might be product related. It could be team related. It could be anything really, but eventually there are going to be milestones that change your business and therefore need to change you as a founder.

You've probably heard some of these sayings before, but I wanted to add a little more perspective to some of these. This leads me to the four stages of founder evolution, stages that every single founder from every single company has to go through.

Stage 1: Working *in* Your Business

We all know the cliché: working *in* your business versus working *on* your business. In the beginning, you are in the trenches, sleeves rolled up, doing the work. You can have all these outlandish ideas of what you want to do with your business, but if you personally are not actually doing the work on a day-to-day basis, nothing is going to happen. In our early days, box packing was the number one "work in the business" task that needed to get done no matter what. In fact, our most important thing in the business was going into the warehouse every day and packing boxes. It was literally the opposite of fun or sexy. It didn't technically "move the business forward," but it was what needed to get done to maintain and operate the business on a day-to-day basis. If you're like me, I struggle a lot with tasks that involve working *in* the business. Not because I have a problem with doing these sorts of things—we all understand that they *need* to get done. But I have struggled with it because, at the end of the day, I always felt like I accomplished nothing. I would get home and feel like, because I didn't go and get a win or somehow move the business forward with a new deal or launch a new marketing campaign, my day was wasted.

Working in the business for me didn't just mean packing boxes. It meant physically going to trade shows. It was meeting our suppliers and picking up product. It was delivering boxes to customers if—for whatever reason—we couldn't ship them out. We used to fill our time with pop-up shops at gyms, off-loading trucks and filling freezers, entering information into Excel sheets, and pretty much anything and everything that needed to get done in a day.

During this phase, as the founder, you arguably need to be the hardest worker, and you're going to be doing the most mundane but necessary tasks possible. This is a tough time depending on your skill set, but if you ever feel yourself slipping into a dark hole where you want to neglect these tasks, use this saying to keep a proper perspective: "We always overestimate what we can do in a year and underestimate what we can do in ten." This is a way to understand that even if you didn't *feel* like you moved the needle forward today, working in your business efficiently is what will set you up for your future wins.

Stage 2: Working *on* Your Business

Once you get to a point where you have either a team or the right systems and processes in place, you're suddenly able to take a step back from the day-to-day and start thinking about week-to-week or month-to-month—quite literally, this means you are working *on* your business. There are a million different ways to approach this stage. Maybe you can finally do more targeted market research or work on the improvement of a process or service. For me, I wanted to dive into Facebook ads when we hit this stage. I wanted to optimize how we got customers in the door. This is the stage where you either physically or metaphorically go from heading to the warehouse each morning to heading to the office.

Stage 3: Working *outside* Your Business

This is when you finally reach that point that not only you but other members of your team are able to consistently work on the business. Maybe now you have a couple of managers or team leads, or maybe it's just one other person. Either way, suddenly you're running a full-fledged business. You have revenue coming in. Maybe you are profitable; maybe you're not. But you have systems and processes, and you have customers coming in. And your team is optimizing all of this. Things are now moving without you having to push every piece forward yourself.

This is the phase where, now as a founder, you can begin working *outside* your business. What I mean by this is at this stage I was spending less time with my team and more time trying to get partnerships with other businesses. It meant trying to get truLOCAL in the media. It meant I could go out there and pitch investors to promote and help support the business.

Stage 4: Working *for* Your Business

This stage was important to me, because now that the business had grown and was rolling along, it was time to dive back into the business. But this time it's not so much to focus on the systems and process; that's already moving along. It's not to meddle with the day-to-day affairs like you did in the early years. This time, when you're diving back into your business, you're working *on* your team. You're working for your team to train and lead them to optimization and efficiency. This is where you start training your next level of managers so they can also run the business efficiently.

Because when you think about it, how else do all of these people get what they need to do their job well? How do they become effective workers? It doesn't just happen organically. The evolution of the team is a direct result of the vision of the founder. An example of this is communication. How are sixty people communicating with one another? Is it via email? Maybe a platform like Slack? How many meetings are in-person? How many are via Zoom? These are all really important things to figure out.

And it's not only regarding how you communicate, but who's going to communicate with whom? Do you have a structure where an issue is routed directly to a subject matter expert? Do you even know what a subject matter expert is? If this is an issue in your business, then it's your job to help remove these barriers so that your team can work more effectively. Working on this type of stuff is a far cry from the skills required to pack boxes or muster up the motivation to do the same mundane tasks every day. But making the transition from being the best at the former to being the best at the latter is all part of your transitions and journey as a founder.

> **When you look at all four of these phases, each of them comes with their own challenges, and each requires very different skill sets from the founders. But when you have that foundational determination as a professional problem solver, you will ultimately figure it out.**

When you look at all four of these phases, each of them comes with their own challenges, and each requires very different skill sets from the founders. But when you have that foundational determination as a professional problem solver, you will ultimately figure it out. Nobody can teach you how to do all these things. You're not born with the ability to do all these things. How do you go from being a diligent box packer in your organization to being able to land and pitch your company in investment meetings, to nailing TV interviews, to training managers on how to do their job at a high level? These are all things that you have to learn as you go.

That's the goal of a first-time founder—evolving as the business evolves and fulfilling each required role. No one said it would be easy, but there is no other way. And if you get stuck in one of those phases and you're not able to live up to the required skill set, you're going to run into some serious problems. Yes, to an extent, you can hire around those issues—if you can afford to. But at the end of the day, your role as a founder is always going to change based on the size of the business and the needs of the business. And you need to be the one to make sure to change with it.

But, even if you are able to change with the growing needs of the business, there's still one very real danger—the one thing that causes founders to plateau on their own personal development and therefore slow down the momentum of the business. That danger is not knowing when to make those transitions. When the opportunity for transitioning comes up, it's a really tough time. During this time you have to do the responsibilities of both the stage you're currently in and the stage you want to evolve into as you transition. I teach my managers this all the time. When you want to go from your current position into a higher role, until you backfill that position, you're going to end up having to fill both responsibilities.

When you want to go from working in the business to working on the business, you can't just up and walk away from your current responsibilities. Who's going to do them? I had to pack boxes, work trade shows, deliver orders, respond to customers, do pop-up shops, *and* then also add working on the Facebook ads and higher level marketing initiatives for a while before I could leave the warehouse completely. But knowing when to pull that trigger and start the transition from a particular stage can be hard.

I'll never forget, in the early days we all used to pack boxes together as a team, just the five of us. We would eat together, pack boxes together, and all ride together. Nobody wanted to pack boxes, but we all had to do it. But I also realized that we needed to grow the company. And eventually I realized that we needed to focus more on marketing, which was right in my wheelhouse. I was already doing both anyway. I would pack boxes, go to trade shows, meet with suppliers, and deliver orders during the day. Then once I would get home after a full day of work I'd do Facebook ads in the evening. Soon it got to where doing Facebook ads could be its own full-time job. And that's when I realized at that particular phase of the business, my value to the business was to focus on the marketing side.

It sounds like an easy revelation with an easy solution—just stop packing boxes and work on Facebook ads all day. But I felt guilty leaving everyone else in the warehouse to do the job that sucked while I sat in an office. Not to mention it was hard to convince my team that my time was better spent in marketing. So I dragged out my role of packing boxes a lot longer than I should have.

I see a lot of first-time founders in that same situation—they just don't make that hard decision to transition. Regardless of whether it's a political hesitation like it was for me in terms of worrying what the team thought, whether it's a lack of a certain skill set holding you back, making you feel like you're going to be bad at this next role, or whether it's just fear of being able to take on the extra responsibility and it's making you uncomfortable, if you want the business to succeed, you need to evolve and evolve quickly.

CHAPTER TWELVE

How to Stay Motivated—Part 2

Nothing in a start-up moves forward unless you move it forward.

—IRMA BRCANOVIC

Part III of this book has really been about how, in the mid years of your start-up, everything is just about work. It's about having the horsepower to grind out the daily efforts needed to move the business forward inch by inch, day by day.

I'm going to pick back up on my experience with purpose and motivation. This chapter is going to talk about the hard truth around being motivated, and it's a harsh one. In chapter 4, I talked about my experience with purpose—how I found it and what it did for me, how at the time it was hard to actually articulate or even understand what was happening. But being able to look back and realize that football gave me something to strive for, in a way I had never experienced, gave me the motivation I needed to put in whatever work necessary to fulfill that purpose.

I think most importantly, in chapter 4, I talked about how purpose is one of the strongest influencers of motivation. It's what will give you that consistent and prolonged supply of motivation. And we love motivation, because as soon as motivation strikes, not only does our productivity increase, but the urgency in which we tackle a project—and the quality of our work—tends to improve as well. When we're motivated to do something, you give it everything you've got. I don't have to spend too much time diving into what being motivated does for you, because no doubt, at some point in time, you've been highly motivated to get something done. You've also probably experienced firsthand the differences between working on something when you're motivated versus trying to milk that extra effort when you're not.

However, this chapter is where I want to talk about the ugly side of motivation. For those of us who are fortunate enough to have found purpose in our businesses, simply thinking that because you've found purpose and the proportional motivation that comes along with it—assuming that you'll ride the waves of success easily isn't a reality. Even with the most powerful sense of purpose, nothing will keep you motivated 100 percent of the time. *Nothing*. Purpose might be the difference between being in a motivated state 40 percent of the time versus 30 percent of the time, which, when compounded over time, is a significant increase. However, it's still not *all* the time. There will still be times when you lack any motivation to do work; you'll want to neglect your responsibilities and that starts making way for procrastination. This is where you need to learn that, contrary to popular belief, even if you're not feeling motivated, you still need to work. Not being motivated does not give you an excuse not to show up.

As great as motivation is, it's important to see it for what it is. Motivation is a drug. When it's there, you are superhuman and think you can do anything. But when it's not, you crave it. You make excuses as to why you need it, how you can't possibly function without it, how if you only had it, everything would be okay. Be honest with yourself: How many times have you had a list of things to do—you know they need to be done, you know it's important that these things get accomplished in a timely manner—but, instead of just doing it, you wait? You wait for the motivation as though motivation is some sort of limitless pill or lightning bolt, and if you wander around long enough, it will strike you. You do this because you know how you are when you're motivated:

1. Your work quality will improve.
2. You'll actually be in the mood to do it.

But what does that really mean? Does that mean we just sit around being unproductive until motivation strikes? Maybe, but that's a dangerous way to approach business. If you let your motivation levels control your work ethic and overall output, then you're doomed to spend more time searching for motivation than actually working on your business. And that never-ending search for the fleeting kick of motivation is the number one reason a great many first-time founders waste time procrastinating.

> If you let your motivation levels control your work ethic and overall output, then you're doomed to spend more time searching for motivation than actually working on your business.

Want to know how to tell if you or someone else is using a lack of motivation as an excuse? They'll often say things like, "As soon as I ..." or "If only I had ..." or my personal favorite, "I just need to X, and then...." Understanding that you do better work when you're motivated is okay, but using a lack of motivation as an excuse to not do any work is, in my eyes, the number one sign that you're NGMI (not going to make it) as a first-time founder.

When I'm looking at founders to invest in, there's a lot of things I'm looking for outside of the business fundamentals or market. I'm looking to see if the founders have a chip on their shoulder, something to prove, or someone to prove wrong. Being persistent and determined, even stubborn sometimes, are all traits that I see in myself and want to see in the founders I invest in. But something I always want to challenge them on is their work process when they're not motivated. I want to see if they (1) have an understanding of the relationship between motivation and productivity, and (2) if they have a process for working through their own dark times when motivation is hard to come by. This usually turns into an out-of-the-box conversation and acts as a great way to get to know one another on a deeper level outside of the usual business talks. I'd say about 40 percent of founders I talk to have a strategy for this. But if they don't, that's usually the first thing I'll try to coach them on.

It sounds harsh, but as I've talked about before, being successful specifically as a first-time founder, when absolutely everything is working against you, is a game of consistency and attrition. Who can show up every day to outlast and outsmart the others? Nobody cares about your excuses. Once again, not to be harsh, but literally *nobody cares*. Your customers, team, bank account, investors, competitors— you could have the greatest excuse in the world, but those stakeholders aren't going to stop doing what they're doing to console you. Things are going to continue to move forward around you because, in the business world, things are still moving whether you're influencing them or not. The overall market doesn't stop and take a break when you're having a bad day, week, or month. That's the tough part about business; that's why it's so hard to have a work-life balance. And that's why you need to get past that mentality if you want to win.

Everything keeps on moving, and it's your job to stay ahead or, at the very least, keep up with it. Purpose will give you a shot in the arm of motivation. Motivation will make it easier to wake up and do what you need to do. But your responsibility as a first-time founder to yourself and your team is to still show up each and every single day, even when you don't want to.

I'm saying all this, but to use an actual example, ever wonder why they say, "When it rains, it pours"? I truly believe it's because, typically, when one bad thing happens, we tend to start slacking on our other responsibilities. Something punches us in the face, so we decide to take the rest of the day off to crush some cookies and watch Netflix. We let our emails pile up for the rest of the day and start ignoring calls. By the time we wake up in the morning, we've realized that another emergency has popped up right on the heels of the thing that put you on your ass the day before. You reach out to your team, asking why nobody let you know, and they said they sent a number of emails last night to notify you. So, is it true that when it rains it pours? Or did a lack of motivation cause you to ignore your emails, leaving the door open for a compounding issue to grow?

For me, I experienced firsthand what would happen if I decided not to show up even when I was in the absolute darkest point of my time at truLOCAL. This was the first real life or death situation for truLOCAL—quite literally—and has possibly become the most formative singular event in truLOCAL history under the original management. The team internally started referring to it as the "Twelve Days of Phoenix."

For companies that rely on a web or mobile app or shop to run their business, they understand the key role that their platform plays in them being able to operate on a day-to-day basis. truLOCAL was no different. In the early years, I made a commitment to build our site from the ground up and avoid using any of the out-of-the-box solutions like Shopify or WordPress. I took a lot of heat for it, but in 2016, I saw what was happening. Meal kits, grocery delivery, and pretty much any form of online food delivery was becoming a commodity. Every experience was the same—everything from the products, the packaging, the branding, and the websites. I knew we had to find every possible way to stand out, and our website was no different. I felt that if we built our website from the ground up, it would help give our brand a different feel and experience to what our customers were used to from other competitors in the market. It paid off. From 2016 to 2019, our website was unlike anything else on the market. When we would run surveys, customers would actually quote how our web experience was a big factor in them giving us a shot.

With that being said, building a platform from the ground up had its challenges. In order to provide a more unique experience, the trade off was that we lost the benefits of open-source products that played friendly with one another or that had robust documentation to help with quick bug fixes. Because of this, we spent a lot more time and money on our website than most others. To help save costs, and because at the time we didn't have the resources or skill sets in-house to manage our own development team, we used a third-party development house (dev house).

For two years things were as to be expected. We had our typical ups and downs of working with an agency. But overall, the experience was great until we reached a point where our daily needs from the web app started to exceed the time our agency was able to dedicate to it. By this point, we were on daily calls with the agency and had racked up a three hundred-plus to-do list of items which we aptly named the graveyard, because we knew we'd never be able to get through all of them. The "graveyard" was where "nice to have" features and updates would go to die. We were looking to add features at a rate that made it so that we never had time to actually go back and fix minor bugs or issues that would come up, and instead we'd just throw Band-Aids on the cracks that were starting to show.

We'd look to move a button on our website's home page, and next thing we knew, products were being dropped from customers' accounts. On customers' accounts, we'd look to add promo codes to their orders, and we'd find out we broke a link to a product page somewhere. It was getting insane. We were at the point where we were experiencing technical debt at its finest.

For those that might not know, technical debt is the idea of adding quick fixes to your code or just putting a Band-Aid over the problem instead of doing a proper diagnosis and fixing the core issues. Overtime, technical debt adds up, and eventually all of the small issues that you've put off over the months combine into a critical failure, because you haven't addressed the actual problem. It's the technical version of death by a thousand cuts, and it's called technical debt for a reason—it always needs to be paid back. Either you take the time to fix the issues properly along the way, which means you move a little slower and spend a little more on development, or you loose your whole system and have to start from scratch due to a full crash.

It got to the point where we had accumulated so much technical debt as we grew, and the needs from our website had changed so much from when we initially built it that it just made more sense to rebuild from the ground up. If we were going to do this, we figured we were finally at the size and finally had the resources to build out our own dev team in-house.

We started by putting up job postings, looking for a lead developer to come up with and scope out what it would look like to rebuild our custom platform in-house. After a month or so, we had a couple developers and a plan that would have our new website up and running in six to eight months. The whole overhaul would be done in two parts: part one, the first part we'd start tackling, was focused on our back-end system, while the second part would focus on the front-end of our website that our customers interacted with. Our whole team was hyped, because our back-end system was where we operated the entirety of the business. Everything from our CMS (content management system), CRM (customer relationship managment), product management, and every other aspect of truLOCAL, had built up so many bugs that—I kid you not—50 percent of our operational time was spent investigating why all sorts of anomalies were happening, rather than actually working on new projects. Because of this, we decided to name our new back-end system Phoenix, a nod to the mythical bird that would burst into flames and be reborn from the ashes of its previous self. The thought process was that our back-end system Phoenix was going to rise from the ashes of our old system.

Not only did we need to completely rebuild our platform from the ground up, which took time and planning, but the most important part was the migration. Essentially, the migration meant that we needed to transfer all of our existing data from our current website that the agency built for us over to the new platform our in-house team built. If this sounds simple, it's not. Not only does everything have to match up perfectly from a database perspective, but the piping required to actually facilitate the transfer of this data also needs to be perfect. Any misstep or miscalculation could lead to lost or corrupt data, and when you're a subscription-based business, losing data and having to reach out to customers to have them resubscribe is a major risk.

About ten months after we started the project, we were ready to make the transition. I'll never forget this day because it was October 31, 2019—Halloween. We needed to bring our current website down for a couple hours to begin the migration, so we decided to do it at 3:00 a.m., when there was a low likelihood of anyone being on the website. We let most of the team sleep, seeing as it was really just something that our dev team had to deal with. So I met up with them at the office around 2:30 a.m. to begin the transfer. At the time when I left, it seemed like everything was moving along pretty well. The team was in high spirits, and everyone was excited to finally have part one complete and start using Phoenix.

By the time the rest of the team started to file into the office, everything seemed to be a success. The migration was complete, and our developers who came in at 3:00 a.m. to start the migration headed out for some much deserved rest. It wasn't until midday that we started to notice something was wrong.

Our consumer experience team is always our first respond-ers when it comes to any issues that customers might be having. It makes sense. When customers are experiencing some sort of issue, they message in to our CX team. By around 5:00 p.m., they started noticing a huge influx of abnormal customer issues pouring in.

We didn't notice it at the time, but these were the first warning signs that our migration had failed. Over the next twenty-four hours, we would start to become overwhelmed with hundreds of customer issues. We were in a situation where customers who had canceled years ago were receiving notifications that their orders were about to be billed. We had situations where customers were receiving two, three, and in one instance *six* duplicate orders that showed up at their door. There was no rhyme or reason to the topics that were coming in, but they were coming in fast. We literally couldn't keep up with the number of issues, and for the first time in truLOCAL history, we took down our website.

It was a dramatic blow for us, but the worst part is that taking down the website didn't even help. Sure it stopped new orders from coming in and prevented customers from making changes to their account, which obviously weren't being recorded on our end. But it didn't do anything about the fact that our back end was randomly scrambling orders, billing cards, and locking customers out of their accounts without our control.

We were in a race to untangle what was going on and find out what was causing all of these triggers to occur, while at the same time trying to calm down the hundreds of customers who were threatening to cancel. We were in a full-blown, code-red crisis.

Seventy-two hours in, and we still didn't even know where to start because we didn't even know what was wrong. Was it the front end? Was it the back end? Was it the database? What was causing so many different types of issues to pop up? By this point we had all hands on deck. We spent the first three full days staying, eating, resting, and showering at the office just trying to problem solve. After the first three days, when we literally had to force ourselves to get some sleep, we were leaving the office no earlier than midnight and showing back up at 5:00 a.m. to keep triaging.

The Twelve Days of Phoenix will always stay with me, because things had gotten so bad that it was the first time I actually thought to myself that this might be the end. I didn't know how we could come back from such a disaster like this. Our customers could only forgive us for so long, and it had already been three days with no progress.

We were going to churn out all of our customers, and that was going to be that.

It was the lowest I'd ever been. I just wanted to crawl into a hole. I had no idea what to do, and because I actually thought it was the end, I for damn sure didn't feel all gung-ho and motivated to spend twenty-two hours at the office spinning around in circles, owing my team answers that I didn't have.

Over the next couple days, we found out that Phoenix didn't properly connect to the front-end of our website, meaning that when the customers who were actually able to logged into their accounts to edit box contents, billing details, or shipping dates, none of those changes were being saved. We also found out that the migration where we pulled all the data from our existing website and funneled into Phoenix also failed, meaning that we didn't know what data our new system had and what data was missing.

It got to a point around the six- or seven-day mark where we realized if we wanted to get a handle on things, we needed to stop the chaos. As we continued diagnosing, it became apparent that our old back end, our new back end, Phoenix, and our payment processor, Stripe, were all competing for control. Our old system was built in a way that Stripe was what would determine when and how customers' subscriptions were set up and billed. Whereas Phoenix was architected in a way where Phoenix would assign the rules and simply tell Stripe who to bill and when.

Our current strategy for trying to fix our issues was to slowly untangle and unhook broken system after broken system one at a time. But it got to the point where the process was moving too slowly, and more issues were coming up faster than we were solving them. What this meant for us was that we needed to make the most intense decision truLOCAL had faced up to that point. To fully stop this mess, we needed to remove all our subscription data from Stripe and let our new system take full control so that we could start to build back. But this also meant that if Phoenix wasn't working properly and didn't accept our subscription data, then, because we removed the subscription data from Stripe, we would have essentially lost all of our customer data and, therefore, all our customers. Pure game over.

Before asking the obvious, no. There was no quick or easy way to back this data up or reset it once we pulled the trigger. Eventually, I called the shot, and we cut the cord with Stripe.

Making that decision was definitely a moment for me. It was a binary decision that would give me immediate feedback as to whether it was right or wrong. A few moments later, we would either see Phoenix take over and start to push through transactions, or we would wait, and wait, and wait, and eventually swallow the reality that no transactions were being pushed through, and therefore it would be the sign that our customer data was lost. At the time, I didn't post much on social media, but in November 2019 I actually posted a picture on my @darkmarc_ Instagram of the code that was written to execute the command and captioned it "what doesn't kill you, makes you stronger" to serve as a reminder of that moment for me. Thankfully, through the combined team effort of our CX team, dev team, ops team and fulfilment team, our fixes took hold.

It didn't get us out of the fire, but by day eight we had disconnected the system that was causing all of the sporadic triggers, so we were finally able to make meaningful progress on our list of issues. It took twelve days in total, where we were pretty much living at the office, wondering if we'd even have a business the next day. Twelve days until we finally got our system to a point where we could breathe.

I don't have the skill as a storyteller to properly articulate what we went through as a team during those twelve days. To watch everything you built over four years be potentially burned to the ground in just under two weeks is a reminder to always appreciate our lack of control over things. But like I wrote in my post, "what doesn't kill you makes you stronger." That saying definitely stood true for us during this time. I watched the team rally in a way that I had never seen before. Team members from across every department rose up and filled in when we needed them to help get us through. We had customers and suppliers reach out when they got wind of what was going on to lend a helping hand or just say they were rooting for us. And for me personally, it taught me the importance of working even when you don't want to.

In the first few days when I thought all hope was lost, if I had just crawled into that hole and gave up, if I just went along for the ride instead of pushing back on the forces trying to impose their narrative of how our story should end, then most certainly truLOCAL would have died in 2019. If I only worked when I was motivated, I would have stayed home and waited until my pity party was over and then gotten back to work after I felt refreshed and rejuvenated. But by that time, our customers would have moved on, our team would have felt abandoned, and our competitors would have smelled blood in the water and made headway in grabbing our outflowing customers.

In this scenario, my feelings didn't matter, and my burnout didn't matter. I couldn't tell Phoenix my problems and hope it felt sympathy for me. It wasn't motivation that got us through. It was understanding our responsibility to each other, to truLOCAL,

> It wasn't motivation that got us through. It was understanding our responsibility to each other, to truLOCAL, and to our customers that got us through. Motivated or not, we needed to show up.

157

and to our customers that got us through. Motivated or not, we needed to show up.

It's a hard pill to swallow. And I wish there was a more eloquent or step-by-step way to describe this, but it's the same as trying to tell a professional athlete how to dig deep in the fourth quarter. Nobody can teach you that. You can learn and perfect the skills required to perform in that situation, but the willpower it takes to look inside and pull that out is a personal journey—only you can do that for yourself. Like I said at the beginning of this chapter, working even when you're not motivated isn't supposed to be a rah-rah-toxic-work-bro rallying cry. It's just truth, and it's just a fact of business, and part of life for a first-time founder.

PART IV

All That Matters Is Using What You've Built to Your Advantage

CHAPTER THIRTEEN

If You Can't Communicate, You Can't Lead

The art of communication is the language of leadership.

—JAMES HUMES

As you get into the later years of running your business, you're now deep into the finessing stage. You're pulling the strings from afar and using your leverage to not only get more done but also get it done more efficiently than if you were to do it yourself or without your team.

At the beginning of the book, I talked about how problem-solving is the single most important skill you're going to need to get off the ground and be successful as a first-time founder. But now as you and your business have grown, there's another skill that you're going to need to embrace, whether you're comfortable with it or not: facilitating communication.

Your business is off and running. Things are starting to get a little smoother. It's not that you don't have any problems.

> If you want to be a leader with finesse, you need to understand the strengths and weaknesses of your team.

However, the problems you do have, you're dealing with differently. These problems go beyond grinding it out and being a professional problem solver. These problems are actually so big that you really do have to tap into all of your resources. And to me, if you want to be a leader with finesse, you need to understand the strengths and weaknesses of your team.

By this phase, you hopefully realize that you can't have your eyes on every single problem. You need to make sure that all your team members are looking out for problems as well. But you also need to make sure that they're sharing information with one another. After all, information is king. And if you have a lot of really, really good people in place, but all that information is either stuck with them because they don't know to share it, or when they do share it doesn't end up in the right person's hands, or you just simply haven't set up an efficient way for communication to be spread throughout your business, you have a serious issue.

That's why one of the most impactful things that you can do at this stage of your business is facilitate smooth communication channels throughout your organization. Trust me, this sounds a lot easier than it actually is.

There are a few very tangible benefits that come along when you have proper communication channels in place:

1. It will increase the speed in which problems are identified and therefore how quickly problems can be addressed.
2. It will increase productivity, especially when multiple teams or departments are collaborating on a specific project.
3. By making it easy for your team to communicate, it will help foster ownership, community, and culture by making sure everybody feels heard.

In my opinion, communication is the key to everything in life. But unfortunately, in today's society, not many people know how to properly communicate. It's not our fault—we've evolved into a world where interacting on complicated and nuanced topics is now reduced to 144-character limits and emojis. We place so much weight on words said and not enough weight on the overall intent of the message.

When you think about it, English speakers are already at a disadvantage because the English language in general is a horrible means of communication. We have one of the few languages that is actually a composite of nearly a dozen other languages, many living (like French and German) and many of them dead (like Old Germanic, Old English, and Latin). That means we have a lot of different words for the same thing. So right off the bat (the kind in baseball, not the nocturnal mammal), we have issues that cause confusion, not to mention the intonation assigned to each word and how that translates over email or social media. You ever have someone take your text the wrong way?

I'd also argue that if you really take a look at it, a majority of life's problems can be attributed to miscommunication. How many wars have stemmed from a communication breakdown? How many divorces were filed because of feelings left unsaid? How do you even start to tackle this? Not only with society but with the history of our language working against us, how can we possibly hope to avoid needless conflict caused by miscommunication?

The fact is miscommunication is inevitable. Based on this premise alone, it should become obvious how important it is for you to not only be a good communicator yourself but also how important it is for you to focus on making sure your entire team is communicating well. So as a first-time founder, step one is understanding this and doing everything in your power to educate and foster the strongest possible communication practices you can.

Here are three things to focus on if you want to improve your chances of having good communication practices among your business.

Overcommunicate as a Leader

A lot of people hate to overcommunicate because they feel like they're on a rant. But believe me, it's better for your team to think you are ranting than having them misunderstand whatever point you are trying to get across. When you need to get a task accomplished, the last thing you need is to have someone say they didn't understand what you really wanted. If you're consistently running into a situation where things aren't being done the way you wanted, you need to start looking in the mirror first.

I always like to be very clear and specific on the things I'm looking for. I have no shame repeating myself, and I highly recommend that people repeat themselves as much as possible. There's also nothing wrong with having people repeat the information back to you. This might sound like overkill, but until you build that relationship with someone, or a team of people, you need to make sure your message is received.

You know how people say they can finish each other's sentences? That's a skill that takes time to develop—it doesn't just happen organically. And until you get there, you need to overcommunicate.

Call Out Etiquette for Your Communication Tools

Even prior to the pandemic, we lived in a world where we were sending out emails and texts and using platforms like Slack and Zoom to communicate. We all know it's very difficult to get intonation across when it comes to digital communication. How many times can you think of where someone got personally offended at the tone of someone's email, even though there was no bad blood or offense intended?

These little miscommunications are a waste of energy and can be avoided. When choosing and setting up your communication tools, it's more likely than not your team knows how to actually use programs like Slack, Outlook, or Zoom. But based on what I talked about previously in terms of miscommunication and the weight placed on words said, you shouldn't just assume that everyone is on the same page in terms of how to interpret messages from that given platform.

You should also teach your team what to expect from these channels. If you're a direct and to-the-point messenger, for example, take two seconds to let your peers know that in advance. Simply explaining to someone that your communication style is to respond quickly and in brief sentences lets them know that if they receive what feels like a sharp message from you, they know not to dig too deep into it. Tell them that they can be direct back with you and that they can openly and freely ask if they ever need clarification on something or are worried that you're disappointed with them. Just addressing this in advance can avoid a lot of potential resentment. This is especially important when bringing on new team members. When you're onboarding, it might be worthwhile to give them a heads-up that the "Thanks. *Period*" isn't actually sassy. I still do this to this day—I'll send out a message to my team and remind them not to take Slack or email messages personally. I'm a quick and direct messenger. When someone sends me an email, I'll have a short response. I don't add a lot of fluff.

Honestly, this might sound ridiculous to some of you. I get it. As someone who believes that nowadays people are too easily offended by everything anyway, why are we going out of our way to make sure people aren't getting offended? Well, it's because regardless of your feelings as a founder, if people on your team are getting offended or missing actionable items in messages because they didn't understand, that is going to directly impact the efficiency of the business. That alone makes it worth addressing.

Communication across the Business

Lastly, it's piecing all of this together to make sure that the flow of information across the business is as frictionless and fluid as possible. The last thing you want is to be running a siloed organization. What that means is that you do not want a situation where you have departments that only communicate internally. As businesses tend to get larger, they tend to get more and more siloed, leading to them only communicating within their own team or department. Team members need to be encouraged to reach out across departments if they need help or have a question. By overcommunicating as a leader and making sure you not only have the tools but also making sure your team knows how to use and interpret those proper tools, you'll be giving yourself an advantage against competing founders and businesses who get bogged down and struggle with the dark holes that can be caused by miscommunication.

> Ensuring and facilitating clear communication is one of the most important things you'll ever do as a first-time founder, because you can't do everything anymore.

Ensuring and facilitating clear communication is one of the most important things you'll ever do as a first-time founder. This is because you can't do everything anymore. You can't have your eyes everywhere. You can't have your hands in everything. You need to make sure your team can clearly communicate with one another, so that they can make sure to be looking out for the business just as much as you are.

In these later years, your job is now to work for your team. As you start getting better at using finesse to accomplish more faster, you'll realize that to properly leverage and finesse your skills as a founder, you need to have quick and effective communication among all of your team members so that you can move as a unit.

CHAPTER FOURTEEN

You Can't Fake Culture

Real recognize real.

If you think about it, you're sort of the engineer now, working behind the scenes. But the thing is, from what I've seen, there are a lot of early-stage startups that are straight up neglecting culture, or at the very least a lot of them are looking at it as a checkbox to mark off, and move on from. And like I talked about in the previous chapter, communication is a big part of that. But so is a strong culture.

We all know the phrase, "Fake it until you make it." But that doesn't work with culture. Just because you throw some buzzwords on the wall like "Be authentically you through and through," or "Show compassion … always," or my personal favorite, "Nurture, integrity, selflessness … it's who we are," doesn't mean you now have a culture.

> Your culture is the furthest thing from what you plan it to be or what you think it is. Instead, your culture is the actual actions you take.

Ben Horowitz wrote a great book on this called *What You Do Is Who You Are*, and I highly suggest reading it. Long story short, you have to live your culture. Your culture is the furthest thing from what you plan it to be or from what you think it is. Instead, your culture is the actual actions you take. Ironically at truLOCAL, we stumbled on this almost accidentally by ignoring the idea of culture all together for a long time. We were lucky, because we never really had to think about it; we were already living our culture, we just didn't know it yet. I know most places won't be as lucky as we were to have that happen, but it's another testament to why hiring friends is a good idea. Because we already had a ton of respect for one another, you could say truLOCAL actually had its own culture before anybody even decided to label it. We didn't have any trendy buzzwords or anything like that. Our culture was based on the reality that we all worked for one another. That was the easiest way to sum it up. We were a small group of friends that got together in over our heads to try and accomplish something that a lot of people didn't think we could do.

Because of that, and the fact that we had to deal with challenges every single day to stay afloat and prove people wrong, we went above and beyond to help each other. We were all overworked. We were all underpaid. But we all did it because we didn't want to let the person beside us down. That was our culture. And when we hired people, they saw this immediately. They were willing to work harder because they saw the rest of the team doing it, not just saying it.

When I look back, an example that stands out to me was the first year we decided to send out Christmas cards to our customers. In 2016, cards—especially Christmas cards, especially *handwritten* Christmas cards—weren't something people were used to getting from businesses anymore. We figured this would be a great way to go above and beyond to let the few customers we had know that we genuinely cared about them and appreciated their support. We decided not only to send cards to our active customers, but we were also going to send Christmas cards to our canceled customers as well. Because our team was so small, and truLOCAL was such a different concept at the time (remember, food delivery was normal, but frozen meat in the mail, not so much), we felt that it was important to thank *everyone* who took a chance on us and tried the service.

At the time, we probably had about five hundred customers and four people on the team. We ended up making a day out of it and spent the whole day handwriting about 125 cards, each saying something along the lines of "We can't thank you enough for your support during this past year. Without you, we wouldn't be where we are, and we wanted to send this card to let you know how much you're appreciated and to wish you and your loved ones a safe and happy holiday season."

We'd never sign it "The truLOCAL Team" or anything like that— we always signed our individual names. Personally, I always thought this was the most important touch.

I'm not going to lie, writing the cards sucked. The last thing anyone wants to do is sit down and spend a day writing out Christmas cards, but we got a great response our first year. Whether they let us know through email responses or posts on social media, the people who received the cards really appreciated them. Right then and there, we decided that every single year, no matter how big we got, we were going to handwrite Christmas cards to all of our customers.

To be honest, had I known where truLOCAL was headed, I don't know that I would have made the same commitment. What started out as a few friends writing just a couple hundred cards quickly became sixty team members being handed over three hundred Christmas cards apiece to write every December. It definitely wasn't something anybody was looking forward to each year, but we made the rule that if you worked at truLOCAL, no matter how busy you were or how new you were, you were responsible for your share of the Christmas cards. It was a bit of an inside joke to anybody we hired in November. "Welcome to the team. Here's the need to know, here's the team, and oh, and by the way, here's a stack of three hundred cards that we need back ASAP. Have a great first day!"

Since our first time doing it in 2016, we've never missed a year. Even as we almost lost the company to the Twelve Days of Phoenix, we still managed to get our Christmas cards sent out.

The craziest part about all this was that even though nobody liked the idea of having to dedicate their nights and weekends to getting their cards done, it actually became sort of a game. People would get together and strategize on the best way to get them done. Was it twenty-five a night for two weeks? Was it banging out all three hundred in one stint over the last possible weekend? We'd hold contests to see who could get them done the fastest, and we'd run polls to see who everyone thought would submit theirs last. We turned this chore into something bearable—even fun—all because we knew the person beside us was also putting in the work. It was just a small example of how our actions, rather than words, helped shape our culture without actually thinking about it.

As a little nod to our transitions over the year, here's how our Christmas cards evolved from year to year.

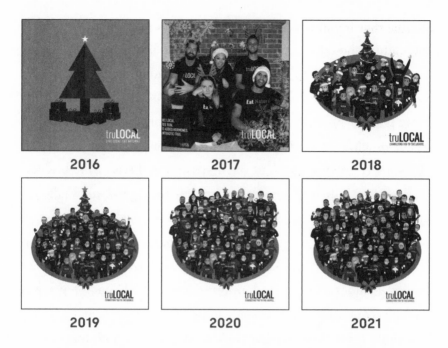

What ended up happening was after a while, as we were hiring new team members, we started getting the question: "How do you describe your culture?" There's a big difference to understand here. It wasn't that we were looking for what we wanted our culture to be, which is where most start-ups start. It was that we needed to find a way to describe and label the culture that we were already living and experiencing.

Once again, the idea here is that culture isn't something you describe and define and *then* live up to. You live it, breathe it, and do it, then reverse-engineer it to understand and better try to articulate it.

Honestly, we were living our culture pretty much day in and day out, so I wasn't in a rush to define it, but I did find this to be an interesting challenge to deal with. I figured if we just sat down and started throwing ideas out there, we might start getting into a bit of an echo chamber, lose our ability to think outside of the box, and maybe, even worse, start to implant or embed expectations on what our culture should become rather than living it out.

So I came up with an idea. I thought it would be a good idea for us to start a book club where we would vote on and read some of the more popular business books. Our goal was one book every month. The book club would actually kill two birds with one stone. First of all, we were growing fast, and the needs and skill sets of the business were growing with it. We needed to start expanding our knowledge, so consistently reading books by and about business leaders like Bob Iger or Elon Musk; marketing, HR, and operations books by managers at companies like Netflix and Pixar; and just overall personal development books by authors like Ray Dalio, Ryan Holiday, and Simon Sinek was a great way to keep the team sharp and keep new ideas flowing.

From there we would get together as a team and discuss the key learning—be it a concept, a sentence, or just a word. We made sure to keep book club attendance supercasual and optional. Usually, we'd have a couple beers and just shoot the shit while discussing what we liked and didn't like and what the main takeaways were. It was important for me to not make this mandatory because when it comes to learning, it's like anything else—you have to want to. If you're forced, it just takes the fun out of it, and I wanted to make sure this was a value add for the team, not just an extra time sink.

Secondly, in addition to the personal development for the team, the idea was that at the end of the year we would have twelve key learnings that we could evaluate and reflect on. From those twelve learnings, the hope was to review them as a team and find which ones we identified with the most. Were

> You're better off not having a culture at all rather than faking some sort of textbook culture just for the sake of having it.

there any that we felt like we related to, that felt real to how we were conducting ourselves and what actions we took on a day-to-day basis? The idea was one that jumped out at us and that we felt a real connection to would become how we describe our culture. To me, it was the most beautiful way to do it because it's not like we were reading those books and then choosing on the spot to be more like the examples we just read about. We were able to digest key takeaways from a dozen books over the course of a year and then decide which ones described our actions most accurately.

I believe in the lyrics that *real recognize real.* This may be a little controversial, but you're better off not having a culture at all rather than faking some sort of textbook culture just for the sake of having it. If you're struggling with culture, try setting up a book club. Take your time; let your culture evolve as you grow and as you bring on more people. Setting up a book club can help you describe and articulate your culture like it did for us.

Remember, there's no guidebook or rule book for business. Find your own reading list that vibes with your team and the culture you're fostering. But as a reference and in case you're interested, at the back of this book I've attached a reading list of the books that we read at our truLOCAL book club. I've also listed in the following bullet points what we choose as a team after our first full year of running our book club. These ideas are the ones that jumped out at us the most:

- Radical honesty. We pulled this from *Powerful: Building a Culture of Freedom and Responsibilty* by Patty McCord, and it represented the fact that we would never let things get lost in translation. If we felt a certain way about something, or ever had something we wanted to say, we would always be radically honest with one another, and we would be stronger because of it.

- Obstacles equal opportunity. We chose this from the book *The Obstacle Is the Way: The Timeless Art of Turning Trials Into Triumphs* by Ryan Holiday, and it was to always remind us that no matter how big or how insurmountable the challenge in front of us seemed, obstacles can always be turned into opportunities, as long as you choose to look at them that way.

- What's YOUR why? We came up with this one from Simon Sinek's *Start with Why: How Great Leaders Inspire Everyone to Take Action*. We choose it as a reminder to always remember why we do what we do, not just how. One of our team members suggested throwing the "Y" in front because it's not just something we do as a collective but also something we should do on an individual basis.

- Don't innovate for the sake of innovation—innovate when you have to. We pulled this from *The Innovation Stack: Building an Unbeatable Business One Crazy Idea at a Time* by Jim McKelvey, and it serves as a reminder to not do things the hard way or the flashy way just for the sake of it. Do things that work, even if they're boring. It's an ode to marching forward and not making up distractions that don't need to be there.

- Feedback is a gift. This one came from *The Making of a Manager: What to Do When Everyone Looks to You* by Julie Zhuo and was one that I personally pushed for. Organizations often withhold productive yet critical feedback because they don't want to have hard conversations, or they're worried about how the other party will receive it. We chose this one to always remind the team that feedback shouldn't be seen as negative and instead should always be welcomed, as long as it's in the spirit of forward momentum and productivity.

CHAPTER FIFTEEN

Being Organized as a Person Who Thrives in Chaos

Edit your life frequently and ruthlessly. It's your masterpiece after all.

—NATHAN W. MORRIS

I've been preaching how this is the time when you need to be working smarter. How this is when you need to accomplish more than any one person could do alone. How your strength and efficiency come from your team, so therefore it's important to make sure your team is operating as smoothly as possible. Transitioning into these new skillsets is key, but I'd be holding back if I didn't also touch on one of the transitions that I struggled with the most.

This chapter is specifically for people who have a hard time with being organized. I am by no means an expert when it comes to this—in fact, I'm the literal opposite. But because of how much I struggled with it, I really want to write about this in case there's anybody else out there who's having the same struggles.

I wanted to accomplish two things with this chapter:

1. Describe my experience coping with the requirement of becoming more organized so that you know you're not alone

2. Giving you a dive into my process to show how keeping it simple might work for you if you struggle with organization

As your team and business gets larger and more complex, so do the moving pieces, and you need to continue to evolve along with it. Sooner than you might like, being organized will no longer be a "nice to have." It's going to be a requirement. If you're like me, these are the words that keep you up at night.

A lot of the things that made me a good first-time founder actually slowed me down in becoming a good operator. I loved problem-solving. I loved crisis. I did well on my toes and typically operated well under pressure. But I think a lot of that came from always thinking *forward*. I was always thinking ahead, trying to be two or three moves in front. I was always thinking about what needed to be done next. Very seldom would I think *backward*. That's the best I can describe it. When it came to reflecting or sticking to a plan by looking backward on what was set out, I would always get distracted with new ideas or try to change plans that were already in motion. I've now come to realize that organization typically comes from looking backward, and in the early days, I was naively fine with being disorganized because I was one of those people who thrived in chaos.

> Sooner than you might like, being organized will no longer be a "nice to have." It's going to be a requirement.

I think the blessing of having some really organized people join truLOCAL early on actually ended up being a bit of a curse for my own personal development because it masked how bad I was at actually tracking progress. For some of you, that's probably a breeze. But for me, I hated the thought of even trying to get organized. I've used every system out there—Monday, Asana, Jira. Name it, I've tried it. Literally, none of them worked for me. Admittedly, my attention span is about as low as they come, but realistically the reason they didn't work was because I didn't stay consistent with them.

In my eyes, when it comes to being organized, an underlying requirement is consistency. Being organized is based on consistently documenting to-dos or progress in a way that even once we forget something, or if it's not at the forefront of our mind, we can reference our documentation as a reminder of what needs to be done. If that documentation is not being consistently updated, or pieces of information are missing, realistically it can no longer be used as our source of truth, which means it starts to lose value as an organizational tool. The way I looked at it was that once that consistency started to slip, it was pretty much game over.

I could mask my own issues with personal organization, but what made things worse was that it's one thing to keep yourself organized, yet it's another thing to also be organized as part of a team or project. When I had to use specific tools or methods as part of a team or group, I'd use them, but I always felt like I was duplicating work, which made it even harder to stay consistent. This affected me, but I

When it comes to being organized, an underlying requirement is consistency.

also noticed that the feeling of doubling up on work was something that affected my team as well. People who were already highly organized and had their own process for tracking projects and to-dos were now forced to do it twice. That's bad enough already, but even worse was when I found out that one team member had actually completely given up on using their own methods of organization to move over to this new platform, and immediately their productivity started to decline. There's absolutely value in having an entire team on the same platform, but at the same time that's like forcing your championship driver to switch cars because you have a new sponsor and then watching their performance drop.

Eventually, it was time to practice what I preached, and I noticed that getting myself organized in a way that made me more productive was something that I couldn't put off any longer if I wanted to continue evolving my skills and transitioning my role as the business grew. It was my biggest weakness, and I needed to tackle it head-on. I started watching my most organized and highest-level operators and what they were doing to stay organized, and the thing that jumped out at me right away was that I noticed all of them used different tools and methods. For some, it was pen and paper; for others, it was some form of organizational platform. After watching them for about a month, I came to the conclusion that, really, there's no be-all and end-all of a formula for organization. To be organized, you need to do what works for you.

As someone who hated organization, after realizing that instead of looking at what other people were doing, I should break down what I personally needed in a tool or system and work backward from there, I was becoming a lot more open to the idea. And that realization alone made me feel like I was making progress. For me, it was all about keeping it easy, simple, and light. By leaning into this, I was finally able to find what worked best for me.

I wanted to start with finding out why I was drawn to something simple and light, and I figured I'd do this by working backward from how I think about problems, come up with solutions, document ideas, and so on. Ideas come into my brain and then immediately back out in about 2.2 seconds—exaggeration, but they do always come to me when I least expect them, and then they don't last long. It's usually when I'm in the shower or driving in the car. Usually, it's just various to-dos like, "Remember to tell so and so about XYZ," or "Still trying to call X person about that quote," or "Don't forget to approve Y design." But other times it was genuine breakthroughs on strategy or solutions to problems that I'd been wrestling with for a couple weeks. Whether it be the random to-dos or the larger breakthroughs, what I did know was that they were always things I wanted to elaborate on in the future.

I used to start off by just telling myself I'd remember them and write them down later, but as you can imagine, that rarely happened. I'd already forgotten the idea, and let's say on the off chance I actually did remember the idea, I wasn't in the mindset or setting to fully elaborate on it. Regardless of the cause, this meant I'd usually lose out on recording some of my best ideas, or random small tasks would slip through the cracks.

In retrospect, when you're looking back on a lost idea trying to remember it, for some reason your mind does a great job of inflating the importance of that lost idea and has you believing that you lost out on the cure to cancer or the next big technological breakthrough that would skyrocket your business to new heights. While that may not be the case—whether you're losing out on a new color scheme for your website, a product name or tag line, something you wanted to discuss in your next manager meeting—losing one small idea per day every day for a year could leave your business at a fraction of what it could be.

Thinking about these factors added up to me finally getting to the core necessities of what I felt I needed to be more organized. It boiled down to two needs:

1. I needed a way to capture fleeting ideas.
2. I needed a way to elaborate on them in a time that suited me and when I felt I was in the best position to elaborate on them.

If I could find something that would address these two needs, I'd not only be better at holding meetings, completing tasks on time, actioning on new strategies, and overall becoming a better leader, but if I documented all of my thoughts, I'd be building up a database of ideas, concepts, and thoughts that I could reference in the future. So now that I knew what problems I needed to solve, it simply became about finding the tools that would best address those issues.

Because my ideas came to me so quickly, I never had time to open bulky apps. This is where you realize that the difference between one second and two seconds in app time is actually significant. So I figured if I don't need something elaborate, why not just capture the high-level essence of an idea by jotting it down into the Reminders app on my iPhone. It started to work. No matter where I was or what I was doing, if an idea would come into my head, I would take exactly one second to open the app and about another five seconds to write down high-level key words or maybe a sentence about what I was thinking.

As you can see below, it didn't need to be elaborate or have context. It was just to act as a nudge or prompt for me to remember what I was thinking about. These are about 10 percent of the actual current reminders I have had my phone at the time of writing:

- Mitch and Alen community management for Discord
- Tattoo of a mirror
- Add $500 for Lucas to investment spreadsheet.
- "Here's to everybody that understands winning decisions are made five years in advance."
- Extremely focused "call to adventure" will make a huge difference.

The key here was consistency. I promised myself that I would write everything down. I knew that if I only did it sometimes, I'd miss out on the overall value of doing this. And if I felt I was doing a half-assed job, it would end up the exact same way as when I tried to use other methods. After about a week of writing down everything that I thought was worth remembering into my Reminders app, it stuck. This free app on my phone solved the problem that I'd been struggling with for years. And some companies were charging hundreds of dollars a month for it. I was pretty excited about knocking off the first core necessity of needing to find a way to catch fleeting ideas.

The next part is what really proved to me that choosing how to be organized is a personal preference that has to be tailored to your wants and needs. Reminders is great for high-level ideas, but it isn't where you want to store deep thoughts, concepts, or strategies. Every other day or so, I found myself looking at these initial thoughts in my Reminders app and wanting to elaborate on them further. I wanted something simple. I didn't need a ton of features. I just needed it to open fast and be searchable. Seeing if lightning could strike in a bottle again for me, I figured if Reminders on my phone worked, why not just check out the Evernote app as well? So I did. When I had some time, I'd take what was in my Reminders app and flesh them out in my Evernote.

From the previous examples, here's how I would address them with Evernote:

- Mitch and Alen community management for Discord.

  For this, I would file it under my truLOCAL NFT notebook in Evernote:
  - "One of the biggest challenges we're going to have with getting an NFT project off the ground is nurturing the community on a real-time basis. I'll need to find dedicated individuals who not only bleed black and green but also know Discord. Mitch and Alen would

be good. I'll start with checking in on their Discord background. If it's subpar, I'll fire them off a bunch of resources and get them to enroll in an online Discord course to get the ball rolling. Once this is done, we can look externally if need be."

- Tattoo of a mirror

  This would get filed in the Evernote notebook that I keep for tattoo ideas that I like:
    - "Tattoo of a mirror because, at the end of the day, you're always the person responsible. You can blame anybody you want, but deep down you know and understand that all of the good, bad, and ugly are caused by you. Look in the mirror."

- Add $500 for Lucas to investment spreadsheet.
    - This wouldn't make it into my Evernote app. I would just cross it off.

- "Here's to everybody that understands winning decisions are made five years in advance."

  I have a notebook for quotes that I come up with or that I stumble upon.

- Extremely focused "call to adventure" will make a huge difference.

  This would go into my Web3 notebook:
    - "A call to action is Web2. In Web3 we're looking for a call to adventure. Why are people joining your project in the first place? It's not for a specific action or product;

it's to join a community with a purpose, hence call to adventure."

It worked perfectly because I could make sure to catch all the ideas with Reminders, and then when I finally had some downtime, I could open Reminders and start transferring the ideas over to Evernote where I could elaborate, review them, and even share them if need be. It got to the point where I made it a ritual at the end of my week. I'd make sure that I'd thoroughly review all my reminders in case I missed something and spend an hour or so building out the thoughts and ideas around them in Evernote.

Using my Reminders and fleshing them out in Evernote pretty much became my brain dump. But it also helped me stay organized despite having such a chaotic thought process. I now have a notebook within Evernote for everything, and I keep all notes on a specific topic in the same notebook. My managers' meetings, margin meetings, war room meetings, development meetings, etc. all have their own notebook that I keep adding to. I always have a section in the notebook labeled "next time," which is where I usually toss the ideas from my Reminders app, seeing as they're usually things to discuss next time during our meeting. I have notebooks for my marketing thoughts, my writing thoughts, real estate, Web3, and DAO ideas—pretty much a notebook for every topic I ever think about, and I keep adding to it.

It took me realizing that being organized isn't a standard. You need to build what works for you. By understanding and realizing this and working backward from what my actual needs were as an individual, I feel like I've become ten times more productive.

It doesn't have to be big or complex. It can be as simple as my process or as robust as doing mind maps on your own personal white board. I spent years forcing myself to become more organized in ways that didn't work because I was trying to copy someone else's way of being organized. If this example helps you, then go for it. But try to figure out your own way of staying organized, even if it seems basic or simple. There's no rule book for any of this stuff. Just do what works for you.

CHAPTER SIXTEEN

How to Stay Motivated—Part 3

If you are what you say you are, a superstar, then have no fear,
the camera's here, and the microphone, and they want to know.

—LUPE FIASCO

I want to wrap up with my final thoughts on how to set yourself up to survive the long haul of being a first-time founder. As you've guessed, I put a lot of emphasis on the relationship between purpose, motivation, and the ability to produce the work you need to win.

We've come to terms with the fact that, even as you progress along your journey, things don't get easier. Instead, you have a lot more power and resources at your disposal to deal with your problems. The focus now is less on literal labor and horsepower and more on strategy and finesse.

Ironically, your journey has come full circle, and now you're relying heavily on the skills you started your journey with—problem-solving and decision-making. By this time, you've become a pro, and you've probably also realized how having a clear mind can help you tap into the wealth of experience you've gained by getting to this point to help you problem solve at an even higher level. Whether it be the speed in which you problem solve, the way in which you recruit or tap into resources while you problem solve, or the level of creativity you're able to conceive while you problem solve as a highly leveraged founder with the ability to make a cascade of action occur with a single email, your mind has become your most valuable asset. Being able to get the most out of that mind should now be your number one priority.

This is where the power of self-awareness becomes key. At this stage, you need to be able to understand what gets you going, what gets you operating at a higher or lower level than usual. What I mean by that is you need to be able to engineer your mood and work ethic. The journey is too long and filled with too many challenges to just ride the sporadic ups and downs of emotion and hope that you'll feel up to the challenges when they arrive. You've got to understand yourself to the point that you instantly know when you're feeling down or out, or when you know you're about to have an unproductive week due to lack of motivation. You need to be able to identify that and proactively respond. This journey requires you to be the best version of yourself, and long-term motivation and productivity do not just happen by chance—it's engineered.

> This journey requires you to be the best version of yourself, and long-term motivation and productivity do not just happen by chance—it's engineered.

In chapter 12, I linked this to trying to teach an athlete to dig deep in the fourth quarter. You can't teach that; all you can do is just hope that he or she is prepared enough and wants it enough to go the extra mile. That's the same with you as a first-time founder. You are literally the professional athletes of the business world. With these three chapters on purpose and motivation, my hope is that hearing some of my thoughts might help you develop your own personal opinions or principles on how to stay motivated.

So picking up where we left off, purpose is going to give you the best and longest-lasting source of motivation. But even purpose won't give you endless amounts of motivation so that you're motivated 100 percent of the time. Luckily, though, you can supplement this "purpose-fueled" motivation with something I just call "flash motivation."

Flash motivation comes from inputs, actions, or interactions that give you a small, short-lived boost of motivation. We've all been in a situation where having a great conversation with a friend, business partner, or mentor, or when listening to a great speech or watching an inspiring movie left us highly motivated and feeling like a rock star. Maybe it's a beautiful view or your favorite playlist. For a lot of people, it's sticking to a fitness routine, meal plan, or meditation regiment. Regardless of what it is, there's probably a lot of easy things you can think of that make you feel small boosts of motivation. Ironically, however, by the time you wake up in the morning, all that motivation is usually gone—the realities of the world and your daily to-do list set back in, and you're struggling to get out of bed, let alone keep working on your business plan. Hence why I call it flash motivation. That's okay though. The fact that it's short lived isn't a bad thing. We just need to be self-aware enough and realize that we're lucky to even have the ability to generate motivation out of something as easy as a podcast or playlist, or completion of a small task.

When it comes to engineering motivation, there are three levers we can pull to stimulate flash motivation: content, people, and habits.

Content

I'm not going to go down the road of "consume less content." That could probably use a whole book to itself, and there are way better people to help you with that, seeing as I'm an addict myself. Instead, if you're addicted to content and addicted to your screen, at least make it work for you—which is actually a lot easier than you think. The content piece of engineering motivation is the one that had the biggest impact on me because I always looked at my relationship with my screens as relatively negative. During the heavy days of truLOCAL, I'll always remember when people used to ask if I watched TV, and when I'd say yes, I honestly might as well have said that I didn't know how to read or something. It was actually pretty funny. I'll never forget the dirty looks people used to give me when I would say I watched TV every night. At this point, truLOCAL was broadly considered a success, and I had been spending a lot of time doing interviews for large publications on entrepreneurship, as well as giving a growing number of keynote speeches or fireside chats at conferences, so I think I was shattering people's idea of what a successful founder was by saying I watched TV. It was always either a long pause, a snicker, or wide eyes followed by "Really?" and I'd say *yes*.

For me, TV was important. I felt like my days were so heavy, from the moment I woke up and checked my emails until the moment I tried to close my laptop at night. People would constantly come to me for things. Whether it be questions, approvals, problems to solve, things to sign, when you're running the show, the buck stops with you. And that means no matter what, no matter how well insulated you are, no matter how many skilled managers you have, you always have people who need you for something, and throughout the course of the day, it takes its toll on you. Now to be clear, I would never have it any other way. I love being in the center of the action, but it was still draining. My therapy was TV at night. It was a chance for me to literally turn off my brain and just melt into the couch. Most of the time, I didn't even care what I was watching. I would just sit down for an hour or two before bed and wind down as much as possible.

However therapeutic it was, I stumbled upon a way to make it better. I've always loved documentaries—in university *Planet Earth* was my life. Seeing as most of the time I watch TV it isn't necessarily to be engaged every second of the show but instead just to relax, I had no issue watching things on repeat just to have them on in the background. In those early years, one thing I was never very in tune with was how those shows or documentaries made me feel. It wasn't until I found the show *Billions*, which is about two NYC titans—one a billionaire hedge fund manager and the other the US attorney general—and follows their journey as they use every legal and monetary resource a billionaire and a top government lawman would have to take each other down. Long story short, if you like business, the show is probably a good watch for you.

It ended up being one of my favorite shows, and despite being in its sixth season, I found myself drawn back to the whole series at least twice a year. The odd thing was when I started thinking about it, I noticed I would default to watching it when things were going bad in my life. When things were tough at work or I was just in a funk, I always immediately defaulted to putting on *Billions*. I didn't think much of it in the early days, but it didn't take long for me to start realizing why. When I was watching *Billions*, or even just had it on in the background, I felt like I could take over the world. I'll never forget, but I actually used to turn to Irma whenever the main character, Bobby Axelrod, would be a day or two from losing all his wealth and potentially facing jail time and say, "Shit, haha, I guess our problems aren't really that bad." These guys were out here fighting a game of life and death when it came to their businesses at the highest level, albeit fictional, but still. Regardless of what it was about the show, just watching it made me feel better. It made me feel strong, and it always helped pull me out of whatever funk I was in. When I realized that, I started noticing it with other things as well.

Every once in a while, I would catch myself feeling that same sort of inspiration with other sorts of shows as well. I noticed it a lot with Disney documentaries, where they do a deep dive on what it takes to bring the magic to life at Pixar, to see their precision, passion, and dedication. To see how they were all truly at the cutting edge of technology and the work ethic they all brought to the table. I would feel it when I would watch *The Last Dance*, documenting Michael Jordan's historic career and how he didn't give a shit about what anybody thought about it. He was about winning, and he didn't care who he offended on his way there. That definitely did a good job of making sure, during my next day, I was going to kick ass. I noticed it when I would hear Jordan Peterson talk about how every bad decision you make isn't only a betrayal against yourself, seeing as you're damn sure well capable of more, but it's also leaving a door open for worse things to happen to you. That one always inspired me to work a little harder the next day. It didn't even have to be business related. I'm a motor-sport fan, so watching *Formula 1: Drive to Survive* on Netflix gave me that feeling. And even now, most recently, Lin-Manuel Miranda's *Hamilton* has been a pretty strong source of motivation for me.

Once I started becoming self-aware enough to understand what this content was doing for me, it was game over. I turned what I thought was a weakness into a strength, and I started curating all my content. My podcasts, my LinkedIn follows, my Instagram and TikTok, my music playlists, Twitter. At least 80 percent of all those platforms are curated with things that make me feel good, things that make me feel strong.

We digest content nonstop, whether it be on social media, Spotify, Netflix, or YouTube. How can we assume that this doesn't have an effect on our mood? I'd make the argument that we know it does. So instead of letting it control us, let's control it. Use it to help you stay motivated. You're a first-time founder. We're not like the general population. You need every trick in the book to stay strong and stay in the zone. Considering content actually plays a huge role in not only distracting us but actually contributing to negative thoughts and feelings, make sure to flip the script on that and use it to your advantage. Don't listen to that sad playlist when you're feeling down because you want to feel bad for yourself. That's not going to help you. Engineer your content so that it supports you, so that it helps you be better, so that it helps you increase your odds of being motivated.

I don't have the data to support this, but you're a first-time founder and a strong critical thinker, so come up with your own answer to this question. Who do you think is going to have a more productive week based on their content alone? The person who only digests motivational personalized content that they relate to, feel good about, and comes from people they respect and admire or the person who has negative news headlines pushed to their phone and just scrolls through what the social media algorithms decide they should be consuming at the time? Setting up your content so that you get as many opportunities as possible to be exposed to flash motivation doesn't happen by chance. You have to put the effort into it and be disciplined. That's how you engineer motivation with your content.

People

Next up and another one that should be obvious is the people you surround yourself with. You've heard it a million times, and this one is actually true: your network is your net worth. The people you surround yourself with are either going to give you energy, match your energy, or take your energy. The simple answer is to cut out the people who are taking from you or bringing any sort of negativity in your life and add more people who are smarter than you, match or give you energy, or make you feel positive about yourself. Unfortunately, this is easier said than done.

I'm not a relationship manager, so this is one that you need to navigate yourself. But the reason I'm putting this obvious fact in here for you to think about is because, after reading this book, you should be looking at this differently now. You're a first-time founder, and it's your job to set yourself up for success. The people you surround yourself with are going to have a massive impact on your motivation levels. How many times are you around someone you respect, and they just utter something completely random or generic, and you get a boost of motivation? It didn't even have to be that deep, yet it still had that power. Now imagine if you doubled the amount of time you spent around that friend, family member, or mentor. What if by spending more time around them you were picking up more than just random sound bites, and you were actually around enough to pick up key life lessons, learnings, or insights? Increasing your exposure to just one key person could literally change your life just by giving you more exposure to flash motivation and increasing your odds of capitalizing on that.

I have friends who I talk to where, no matter what's going on in my life, as soon as I hang up or we say goodbye, I feel like I was struck by lightning, and I've got motivation for days. (Shoutout to the Sarah Marianos, Reds, Natahan Flannagans, and Jason Browns of the world.) I've also been blessed with the cheat code of life where my wife also acts as that for me, so I'm at a bit of an advantage here. We might not even have talked about business—it's just their energy, optimism, curiosity, open-mindedness, creativity, and ambition.

You've heard about the power of people you keep close to you before, but just for a second take another look at it once you've reached this finesse stage of being a first-time founder. It's your responsibility to engineer your motivation. You can't control your environment, but you can influence it, and you have the power to increase or decrease the positive people in your life.

> You can't control your environment, but you can influence it, and you have the power to increase or decrease the positive people in your life.

Habits

I love looking at good habits as the things you do to keep you on track when you don't know what to do next. They're pretty much a set of principles and actions that you live by so that, even without direction, you're doing things that you know can only lead to positive outcomes. Speaking of using content for motivation, if you're a Disney fan, *Frozen II* has a great song called "The Next Right Thing." Give it a listen if you're ever spiraling.

Flash motivation doesn't just come from the content you consume or the people you surround yourself with—it's also the things that you do for yourself. Your own daily actions are going to play a role in how often you're exposed to flash motivation. The key here is understanding that it doesn't need to be massive wins or accomplishments. You don't need to move a mountain to give yourself flash motivation. You can get small boosts of motivation by just identifying the small wins and then incorporating them consistently into your days. Small wins aren't supposed to be few and far between. You should make "wins" out of things that can happen every day, hence making it easier to turn them into motivation-inducing habits.

It can be as easy as clearing out your inbox, doing your morning meditation, eating healthy for the day, or showing up to all your meetings on time. Whatever your small wins are, it's important that you take the time to identify them and use them as little boosts of energy and motivation throughout the day.

This is why so many people talk about the power of building strong habits. It's not just the fact that they act as rules for your next immediate course of action when you don't know what to do next. It's not just the fact that good habits inherently increase your chances of accomplishing a long-term goal or project. It's not just the fact that strong habits give you a sense of stability in your life so that you can judge your own consistency and progress day by day. It's the fact that good habits also increase your exposure to motivation and therefore increase your odds of productivity outside of the habit itself.

Everybody should incorporate good habits in their lives. But for first-time founders, the advantages are so much more. You need to embrace the wins that good habits will bring. But also, reach deeper—notice the motivation that it brings you. Don't just create good habits to be a better human—your competitors are doing that as well. Go a step deeper and engineer your habits because you want that extra exposure to motivation and then let motivation do what it does best.

At the end of the day, we're human. We're not going to be perfect all the time, and we're not going to be motivated all the time. That's why I even believe in the idea of engineering motivation in the first place—it's to increase exposure. You'll never have a perfect system, but at the very least by identifying the variables in your life like content, people, and habits that can have a really strong impact on your mood and your mindset, you're now able to have more influence over your environment and how it affects you.

This was an important lesson to talk about at the end of this book because, at the end of the day, the world is going to happen to you, and the only thing you have full control over is how you react to it. I said it earlier in this chapter: you can't control your environment. You only throttle up and down the influence you can have on it.

Things like engineering motivation are great, but they're still at the mercy of the world and all the infinite ways things can go off plan. As a first-time founder, the foundation needs to start with you and your ability to deal with everything and anything that might and will get thrown your way. The only time you should try to influence and optimize your surroundings by doing things like engineering motivation is once you've reached the finesse stage of being a first-time founder—once you've mastered your own ability to deal with the world through things like problem-solving and decision-making.

Goddamn Fucking Right

That's it. Genuine apologies if I scared away a few would-be first-time founders. For those of you who did get through this, for those of you who either believed what I said about what you're about to face, or for those of you who related to it because you're already going through it, I truly believe that first-time founders don't get enough praise for the scars they take along the way. We only celebrate founders once they've "made it." We don't salute the bodies of our fallen brothers and sisters who fell along the way. It's unfortunate, but the ones who don't make it far outnumber the ones who do.

This self-imposed grind was supposed to be hard; don't let anybody else tell you otherwise. Don't let anybody else make you feel bad or weird for pouring your soul into this. We choose this; nobody forced it onto us. You deserve a callout for taking your chances. You deserve respect and gratitude for providing innovation and jobs to our country. You deserve recognition for the disproportionate risk you're taking to follow your dream. And I truly hope this book has, at the very least, let you know that somebody out there feels and has felt the same way you do when you're going through your darkest hours. It was supposed to be hard, and you will find a way to power through.

I said it in the beginning of the book, and I'm saying it here again: your challenges in life will always match your ambition.

Never forget, you already have the ultimate weapon at your disposal for the most unexpected and unsurmountable challenge that might come your way. It's you, the first-time founder, locked and loaded, ready to take on the world. My hope is by the time you've finished reading this book, the only thing going through your head after reading that last sentence is "You're goddamn fucking right!"

RESOURCES

BOOK CLUB BOOKS

The Ride of a Lifetime: Lessons Learned from 15 Years as CEO of the Walt Disney Company, Robert Iger

Elon Musk: Tesla, SpaceX, and the Quest for a Fantastic Future, Ashlee Vance

Start with Why: How Great Leaders Inspire Everyone to Take Action, Simon Sinek

The Making of a Manager: What to Do When Everyone Looks to You, Julie Zhuo

My Morning Routine: How Successful People Start Every Day Inspired, Benjamin Spall

Bad Blood: Secrets and Lies in a Silicon Valley Startup, John Carreyrou

Outliers: The Story of Success, Malcolm Gladwell

The Story of lululemon, Chip Wilson

Creativity, Inc.: Overcoming the Unseen Forces That Stand in the Way of True Inspiration, Amy Wallace and Edwin Catmull

Becoming, Michelle Obama

Why We Sleep: Unlocking the Power of Sleep and Dreams, Matthew Walker

Principles, Ray Dalio

Can't Hurt Me: Master Your Mind and Defy the Odds, David Goggins

Launch: How to Sell Almost Anything Online, Build a Business You Love, and Live the Life of Your Dreams, Jeff Walker

The Obstacle Is the Way: The Timeless Art of Turning Trials into Triumph, Ryan Holiday

Powerful: Building a Culture of Freedom and Responsibility, Patty McCord

The Innovation Stack: Building an Unbeatable Business One Crazy Idea at a Time, Jim McKelvey

The Hard Thing about Hard Things: Building a Business When There Are No Easy Answers, Ben Horowitz

PERSONAL READS

What You Do Is Who You Are: How to Create Your Business Culture, Ben Horowitz

Rocket Fuel: The One Essential Combination That Will Get You More of What You Want from Your Business, Gino Wickman and Mark Winters

Delivering Happiness: A Path to Profits, Passion, and Purpose, Tony Hsieh

12 Rules for Life: An Antidote to Chaos, Jordan Peterson

Good to Great: Why Some Companies Make the Leap … and Others Don't, Jim Collins

Lost and Founder: A Painfully Honest Field Guide to the Startup World, Rand Fishkin

The Art of Resilience: Strategies for an Unbreakable Mind, Ross Edgley

The Bitcoin Standard: The Decentralized Alternative to Central Banking, Saifedean Ammous

TV SHOWS AND MOVIES

Billions, StartUp, Silicon Valley, Succession, Halt and Catch Fire, The Smartest Guy in the Room, The Wolf of Wall Street, The Last Dance, 100%: Julian Edelman, The Alpinist, Steve Jobs (2015), *Molly's Game*

PODCASTS

Masters of Scale, The Startup Story, Business Wars, How I Built This, The Joe Rogan Experience

BONUS CHAPTER

Scan the QR code for a link to Web3 introduction.

I wanted to add something that would help keep this community alive. A book is either an interpretation of the past, perspective on the present, or speculation on the future, but regardless of where the focus lies, a book is always a snapshot in time. Once it's printed, it's out. Unless you decide to do multiple editions, it's difficult to update or find ways to continuously add value to your community. That's why I figured, for those interested, I'd add a QR code here that will lead to updated and exclusive content on my web page. I'll be adding resources like "The Bullshit Conversation Checklist" so that, as we keep adding content, you can quickly and easily access it.

It won't all just be about *True Founder* though. There's a lot of things that I find interesting, and I also want to use this code as a way for you to access some of my other thoughts and interests as well.

Some of you might have picked up while reading *True Founder* that I've been leaning pretty heavily into Web3. I truly think that, outside of the speculative value of tokens and PFP (profile picture) NFTs, the tools Web3 provides to enable digital ownership, as well as some of the philosophies that properly structured and incentivized communities are the businesses of the future, are where most first-time founders should be focusing their time. At the time of writing, I have spent about two years researching the space, and I'm excited to start diving deeper.

So the first additional piece of content I want to provide you is my article introducing first timers into my perception of Web3. If you're interested, scan the QR code to find "Introduction to Web3: A Comprehensive Resource Guide for Getting Started."

ABOUT THE AUTHOR

Marc is a University of Waterloo honors graduate who went on to find his niche in entrepreneurship. After two failed start-ups, Marc cofounded truLOCAL and led the business to a successful acquisition in 2020 for $16.7 million.

Marc built the team to sixty-plus employees and expanded across Canada, landing the cover story of *The Globe and Mail's* Report on Business for being Canada's fourteenth top growing company along the way. Over five years, truLOCAL accumulated a series of wins, including a successful pitch on CBC's *Dragons' Den* in 2017.

Marc is a founder at heart and has taken a particular interest in mentoring up-and-coming founders. A series of successful angel investments has helped Marc make a name for himself as a value-added investor among early-stage start-ups. Building a business from the ground up has given him a deep understanding and hands-on experience of what it takes to succeed in a competitive environment, ranging from growth to management development.

Through truLOCAL, Marc set up the "truLOCAL Equal Opportunity Grant," which awarded four Black entrepreneurs with $5,000 business grants. As a Black founder, Marc had become accustomed to having doors closed on him growing up and has spent the past two years empowering minorities to understand that they don't just deserve a seat at the table, but their unique challenges give them an advantage. "We're used to being told no. That's exactly why we're even better prepared to take on the challenges of growing a business."

In addition to sharing this message for companies and academic institutions like Lululemon, Google, FedEx, and the University of Waterloo, Marc has taken a special interest in speaking to today's youth.

If my story can inspire even one kid to take a risk and go after something someone told them they couldn't achieve, then I've done what I'm here to do.

—MARC LAFLEUR

www.marclafleur.com
Instagram: @darkmarc_
Twitter: @marclafleur.eth
Email: letstalk@marclafleur.com
Available for keynote talks